The Cancer Poetry Project

The Cancer Poetry Project

Poems by Cancer Patients and Those Who Love Them

Edited by Karin B. Miller

Fairview Press, Minneapolis

Library of Congress Cataloging-in-Publication Data
The cancer poetry project : poems by cancer patients and those who love them /
edited by Karin B. Miller.
     p. cm.
    ISBN 1-57749-100-9 (alk. paper)
     1. Cancer patients' writings, American. 2. Medical personnel, Writings of, American. 3. Cancer--Patients--Family relationships--Poetry. 4. American poetry--20th century. 5. Cancer--Patients--Poetry. I. Miller, Karin B., 1964-

PS591.C27 C36 2001
811'.54080920814--dc21   00-069184

First Printing: April 2001
Printed in the United States of America
05 04 03 02 01   7 6 5 4 3 2 1

Cover: *Cover design by Laurie Ingram Duren*™

Permissions and acknowledgment for previously published work on page 248.

Publisher's Note: Fairview Press publications, including *The Cancer Poetry Project,* do not necessarily reflect the philosophy of Fairview Health Services. For a free current catalog of Fairview Press titles, please call toll free 1-800-544-8207. Or visit our web site at *www.fairviewpress.org.*

To Thom, whose encouragement and love
have been unending, and who wrote his first poem ever
with Magnetic Poetry during his battle with cancer:

In winter my life was a black mist
The sky was flooded in sad and blue
Then the spring crushed the shadow
and summer's wind blows true.

—Thom J. Miller

ACKNOWLEDGMENTS

Where do I begin to offer my thanks to the hundreds of people who made this anthology a reality? Of course, I begin with my incredible husband, Thom, for his daily strength, his good humor (even in the face of cancer), and his enthusiastic support of me in all my projects – I love you. Thanks also to our daughter, Gabrielle Hope, who inspires us and fills us with joy and love every day. To my parents, Larry and Joyce Bumgardner, and my aunt and uncle, Dennis and Sandra Norlin, who offered both their financial assistance and their confidence that this idea would come to fruition. To publisher and poetry editor Lane Stiles, for believing in the project and seeing it through, with the help of all the hardworking people at Fairview Press, including Steve Deger for his marketing acumen and Stephanie Billecke for her thoughtful editing and lovely book design, plus Laurie Ingram Duren of *Cover design, inc.* for her beautiful cover. Thanks to Geri Chavis for her expertise, multifaceted assistance, empathetic reading, and tremendous introduction. And thanks to Gregory Stavrou at the Virginia Piper Cancer Institute for spreading the word and for arranging a life-affirming poetry performance by ten poets and actors.

Special thanks to my mom, Joyce Bumgardner – educator, creative writing instructor, children's author, poet, and cheerleader – who read, edited, proofread, and offered any and all assistance needed, including babysitting, with unceasing enthusiasm and generosity – this couldn't have happened without you.

A heartfelt thanks to my hardworking and empathetic readers (all of whom have been touched by cancer in some way): Bill Buzenberg, vice president of Minnesota Public Radio; Susan Buzenberg, freelance editor; Nancy Fitzgerald, poet and English professor at the College of St. Scholastica; Betty Fryberger, wonderful family friend; Gaye Guyton, elementary educator and kindhearted sister; Roger Mahn, favorite English teacher of thousands, including me; Ron Robinson, playwright and fave college English professor; Peggy Trezona, psychologist for HealthPartners Riverside oncology clinic; and Lila Weisberger, president of the National Association of Poetry.

Thanks, too, to Suzanne Bluestein of Blue Communications for her media insights and enthusiasm; Brent Kastler for his beautifully designed posters and flyers; Michael Markos for his inviting, user-friendly web site; Craig Purinton of Gilda's Club in New York City for his great insights and advice to persevere; Jean Adams for her wise counsel; Betty Beier of Business Communication and the *Women's Cancer Resource Center Newsletter* for spreading the word; Rod Daniel, Linda Lanza, and others at the National Association of Poetry Therapy for their much-welcomed assistance; *Poets and Writers* for its complimentary call for submissions; and Todd Adams, Wendy Amundson, Mary Divine, Tom Garrison, Cheryl Karpen, Jana Kemp, Karen Kroll, Lissa Reitz, Joel Suzuki, and countless others for their support and networking assistance.

A loving thanks to Peggy Trezona and Ewa Pezalska, and to all the folks at HealthPartners Riverside Clinic who cared so expertly and genuinely for Thom: Dr. Randy Hurley, Dr. Neil Stein, Stephanie McFarling, Carol Jirik, Donna Larson, Mary Traeger, and many others. Thanks, too, to Mary Watson for her great understanding and care, and to Mac Baird for his enthusiasm and kind words.

We will always be thankful for the incredible outpouring of care and love we received from our wonderful friends and family members. They saw us through Thom's cancer and my pregnancy with their frozen dinners, hot caramel rolls, odd jobs and errands, flowers, good books, games, and, most especially, encouraging words, e-mails, and prayers. In addition, they gave their unflagging support as this wonderful project grew out of our cancer experience.

Of course, this book could not have come about without the hundreds of poets who were willing to submit their poetry to *The Cancer Poetry Project*. To those whose poems were selected, please know that your words will never fail to move readers. And to the many more who participated, my sincere thanks for sharing your heartfelt writings. May all of us continue to use our poetry to sustain and comfort ourselves and our loved ones. God's blessings to all.

The Cancer Poetry Project

CONTENTS

POEMS BY THEME

UNDERSTANDING AND COMPASSION

COPING AND PERSEVERANCE

DENIAL

GRIEF

HOPE AND JOY

HUMOR

QUESTIONING

Three years ago my husband, Thom, was diagnosed with testicular cancer. An abdominal tumor the size of a football had taken over one kidney and was threatening his aorta and vena cava. We were devastated. We followed the recommended protocol of surgeries and chemotherapy, gathered our loved ones around us, and asked for prayers. Thankfully, Thom has been cancer free for two-and-a-half years.

At the time of his diagnosis I was in my fifth month of pregnancy with our first child. Just three weeks after his final surgery, I delivered our daughter, named Gabrielle Hope because she was our hope throughout the cancer ordeal. Photographs of the two baldies, our darling babe and Thom from chemo, are both joyful and poignant.

During and after this emotional roller coaster I wrote poetry – fearful, angry, humorous, helpless, and, ultimately, triumphant. At one point, I remember thinking that a book of cancer-related poetry should exist, but I felt sure I could not write one myself.

Then one morning, when Gabi was six months old, I was awakened before dawn by the idea of the Cancer Poetry Project. The details had come to me like a gift from God: I would invite people to submit cancer-themed poetry, then publish the best poems in an anthology.

I could hardly contain my excitement. I strongly believe that this was an assignment, a calling, and I took my assignment seriously. I wrote a proposal, then networked with dozens of cancer organizations and publishers. All of them felt the idea had merit, but no one agreed to take on the project. After nine months I still had no publisher, so I decided to launch the project myself on a shoestring budget. I sent out dozens of media kits locally and mailed hundreds of flyers to cancer treatment centers and universities across the country. The Cancer Poetry Project received immediate coverage by local TV, radio, and newspapers. The director of Fairview Press, Lane Stiles, saw the coverage, understood the project's potential, and offered to publish the book.

In the meantime, the Project had been receiving poetry from around the country. While I had boldly declared to reporters that the goal was to receive at least one thousand poems, the act of opening that first envelope seemed miraculous – there really were other people who coped with cancer by writing poetry.

The submissions first arrived in trickles and streams – five, ten, twenty at a time. Soon the Project received about a hundred poems a week. Initial giddiness at the huge response quickly turned bittersweet at the realization of just how many of us are affected by cancer and how great the need is for this anthology.

You hold in your hands a collection of 140 remarkable poems, thoughtfully selected from the 1,200 submissions received. They are written from a variety of perspectives – patient, spouse, partner, child, parent, sibling, friend, physician, nurse. Taken as a whole, these poems cover the spectrum of emotions encountered throughout the cancer experience. A single poem may inspire hope, hopelessness, anger, heartbreak, humor, or a combination of feelings. One day a poem may affect you profoundly, the next day you'll find another with the exact words that you need. This is not an anthology that you're likely to read in one sitting, but a book you'll pick up again and again – a book that may even inspire you to write your own poetry.

Cancer is not wholly a beast. While it is terrible, many people say they wouldn't want to go back to the lives they were living prior to diagnosis. When faced with imminent death – or the possibility of imminent death – we grieve, we rage, we persevere, we live, and sometimes we die; yet, through it all, the beauty and power of the human spirit seem to grow. The poems in this book are individual acts of courage that lend a voice to this remarkable human spirit. It has been my honor to read and select them.

KARIN B. MILLER

Editor, *The Cancer Poetry Project*

From its inception, Karin Miller's goal for *The Cancer Poetry Project* has been to encourage poetic expression that enhances self-understanding, facilitates the grieving process, and expands public awareness of diverse personal reactions to cancer. Because cancer is a widespread phenomenon in our society, affecting virtually every family in one way or another, a great many people will reap the benefits of this poetry collection. The selections within this anthology represent a kaleidoscope of authentic voices that are relevant to a wide variety of people – individuals at various stages of illness and treatment, families and friends of cancer patients, and the health professionals who work with them. In addition to its range, another strength of this collection is its balance – its honoring of the painful details, the sadness, confusion, guilt, anger, and loneliness, along with its celebration of hope, relief, tranquil restoration, and life's most meaningful moments.

As a professor of literature, a certified poetry therapist, and a psychologist who frequently works with clients facing grief and illness, I have had ample opportunity to witness the powerful therapeutic effects of writing, reading, and sharing poetry. When I was a writing-group facilitator at the Virginia Piper Cancer Institute in Minneapolis, I saw firsthand how creative expression, healing, and support go hand in hand. The force of poetry as an emotional connector and stimulator of insights derives from its personal immediacy, compactness, rich sensory appeal, metaphorical language, patterns, and surprises. Poets tend to combine words and images in ways that make us sit up and take notice. Poetry represents the language of feelings and captures the natural rhythms of our heartbeats, the tempo of our daily lives.

The poems that Karin Miller has assembled here invite us to respond on both a visceral and intellectual level. Readers will listen to soul-searching monologues where individuals confront their conflicting feelings and the meaning of their mortality, or contrast stark hospital walls and the welter of medical technology with soul-feeding fantasies. Readers will hear voices of compassion for loved ones in need. They will journey from past to present to future with people who are grappling with change, assessing their losses and gains, and trying to make sense of their lives.

The poems in this collection function like mirrors, doors, and bridges. Many readers will recognize themselves, find validation for their innermost feelings, and derive comfort from knowing that they are not alone on the road they are traveling. Moreover, *The Cancer Poetry Project* has the potential to lend greater empathy to those who have not been directly affected by cancer and to further sensitize healthcare professionals who interact with cancer patients and their loved ones. As readers, we have the unique opportunity to hear words that women and men carry close to their hearts but often do not say aloud.

The spirit of this anthology is captured in the poem entitled "Poem of the Week." Referring to poems as "strong medicine," "emissaries," and "witnesses," the speaker beckons poetry to "enter the house haunted by illness" and "open the doors shut against fear." I invite all readers of this book to do the same.

GERI GIEBEL CHAVIS

Professor, College of St. Catherine, St. Paul, Minnesota
Vice President, The National Association for Poetry Therapy

POEMS BY CANCER PATIENTS

I ENTERED THE ROOM, NAKED

by Nancy Louise Peterson

finally brought the full-length mirror
to see my back,
shoulder blade to heel,
to see my front,
ankle to stitched chest,
trying to remember how they looked, those nipples,
up to my hair that will be gone, too, in a few weeks.
And I paid closer attention to the crease
in the back of my leg I hadn't noticed before,
the angle of the curve in my back,
the mole at the top of my thigh,
the wisp of hair around my lips.

I raised the jar to the flat of my head
and walked across the hardwood floor,
full of grace.
I caught a glimpse of the swan, her neck movement,
a glimpse of the lioness, her shoulder muscle,
a glimpse of this ancient one, her padded feet,
and I loved her.

IT'S NEVER TOO LATE

by Nancy Louise Peterson

Girls, when you could fit on my lap in the reading chair
we'd find worlds
better than milkshakes
better than haircuts,
where we would go
and words would fill us up
and fall all around our laps.

My daughter women,
sit with me now
when I'm looking for worlds between treatments.
Worlds I can fall into; words I can fall into.
Sit with me in the reading chair
when the sun meets the rooftop
and the chimney smoke seems to stop midair
for the cold and the coming of the dark.
Open the book again with me
to the rabbits' den glowing warm under the tree root.
I will disguise myself and chase you, my little girl bunnies,
into our den, so I can hear you say,
"Shucks, I might just as well stay where I am
and be your little bunny."

And, later, perch with me at the top of the tall white pine.
Help me search for the heron
across the meadow toward the sea.
We will climb to the top
and love the feel of the wind and the sound
it makes through the boughs.
I need to tell you, I've learned both at the same time,
that time is limited
and it's never too late.
I won't give in to the too cold or the too dark.

"Look! There she is!"
The heron moves above the grasses heading out to sea.
"Go!" I cry to her. "Go!"
"I will not tell the hunter where you are or where you are
going." Daughters, come sit with me.
Words will fill us up
fall all over our laps.

*"A big part of my healing from having had breast cancer involved leading
writing groups for cancer survivors," says Nancy Louise Peterson, fifty-four.
"The process of writing 'I entered the room, naked' was cathartic. It allowed
me to reframe my experience, to still love my body and appreciate what I
have – and to love the scars, too." The books she refers to in "it's never too
late" are* The Runaway Bunny *(Harperfestival, 1991), by Margaret Wise
Brown, and* A White Heron and Other Stories *(Candlewick Press, 1997),
by Sarah Orne Jewett.*

Peterson's writing has been included in such publications as Looking for
Home: Women Writing about Exile *(Milkweed Editions, 1990). She also
teaches preschool and special education in Minneapolis, where she lives with
her husband, Chester McCoy. Their two daughters attend Howard University
in Washington, D.C.*

FAREWELL TO HAIR

by Terri Hanson

I stood outside on a windy day
and ran my fingers through my hair.
Long strands of silky threads
blew across the lawn.
They glistened in the sun,
too many to count.

I imagined a nest,
lined with my mane,
woven by a mama bird.
The babies nestled,
snug inside,
warmed by my fallen tresses.

Now on the wintry nights,
when my head is cold,
I pull my wool cap
over my ears and smile
as I dream of baby birds
sleeping in my hair.

"When I first started losing my hair from the chemo, my hair was literally blowing off my head," says breast cancer survivor Terri Hanson, forty-three. "It made me very sad. But then I thought of baby birds sleeping in it, and I thought it would be okay." Hanson heard about the Cancer Poetry Project, wrote her first poem, and sent it off.

"Writing this poem was just the beginning," she says. "Having cancer has taught me that I need to live for today and unleash my creative talents." Hanson has since designed a breast cancer logo, which is being placed on merchandise for breast cancer patients and survivors.

Hanson lives with husband Donald and their three teenagers in Maple Grove, Minnesota. As for her hair, she has kept it short. "People tell me it fits my personality," she says.

THERE IS A RIVER RUNNING IN THE BLOOD OF HIM

by James McGrath

There is a river running in the blood of him
as he tumbles down the mountainside
rolling the stones aside
scattering birds.

A river running in the blood of him
tossing his arms with the reeds and rushes
in the greenest of thunders
and the gold dust of rain.

A river running in the blood of him
murmurs and purrs
when he sleeps
where he sleeps
in the distant places without names.

Oh, the sound.
Oh, the whimper of a river running in the blood of him
      frog voices dark
      escaping as the moon rises
      on a coyote's wail.

Oh, the fury.
The river running in the blood of him
      calling for a response
      from the sun setting
      too early in his daylight.

Only the newest of moons can cup
and hold his tears
running in the blood of him.

James McGrath, seventy-two, has written many poems about his experience with prostate cancer. Six years since his operation, he says he feels great.

McGrath, who lives in Santa Fe, New Mexico, wrote the narrative poetry for the PBS "American Indian Artist" series. A widely published poet, he is also the artist/poet in residence with USIS Arts America in Yemen, Saudi Arabia, and the Republic of Congo.

SUDDENLY, LIFE CHANGES
the diagnosis, 5/17/00

by tommie ortega

i sit on the edge of a cataclysmic abyss
straddling the horizon
on a day made of clay,
as sand dissipates under my feet
and i dream of falling.

BEFORE AND AFTER

by tommie ortega

i remember water
touching my body differently
as, still whole, i lay in that last hot bath.

now i discover a freckle
beneath where my breast once was
and feel a newness come over me.

i ask god to tell me he loves me
and he answers
through the taste of a sweet, summer peach.

water pours over a scarred, curveless mass, and i am cleansed.

Tommie Ortega, forty-six, had a mastectomy immediately after she was diagnosed with breast cancer in May 2000. "As a poet, I have never before experienced an obstacle so numbing that the words would not take shape," she says. "I am not sure if these words succeed. The pieces are still evolving." Through it all, Ortega says, "this experience has taught me how much I am loved, and that the real heroine in all of this is my seventy-one-year-old mom, who was by my side during my entire six-week recovery."

Ortega's poetry has been published in numerous journals, among them Sacred River, Sour Grapes, *and* Chicago House Hotsheet. *She has four self-published chapbooks, including* Paper Napkin Poems *(1992) and* When Angels Sing, I Hear the Blues *(2000).*

Ortega works in human resources by day and is a performance poet by night. She lives in Austin, Texas, with her partner of fifteen years, a poodle, and a mutt.

A WOMAN ARGUES WITH THE CASTING DIRECTOR

by Kathleen A. Rogers

What? What am I doing? What
am I doing here at this audition?

I don't, don't want the part.
I really don't want this part.
I don't, I don't believe it will be glamorous.
It won't be opera, no swooning diva,
no Violetta, no burst of aria.

Even, even if it were, I can't sing.
I never could. And no, I don't, I don't
know how, I don't know how to dance,
to dance with death. You should have
called back someone else.

I fit the part? I fill the bill? I've got the goods?
How could you, could you really need,
another one, another one of me?
A young – well, youngish – female,
one breast of flesh, one something else,
veins full, full of chemo junk, a trouper,
with her very own wig?

I told you – didn't I tell you? –
I don't, don't, don't, don't want
this part. You need someone,
someone else, someone who likes
to lie down on the job. I'm hyperactive,
I really am, I never, never can learn my lines.

I can't believe you truly think
that I'm old enough to play this part.
So call me, call me back, call me back
in forty years. I'll play the old one then
the way I want. I would be very, very good,
I would be very good, very good at old.

Can't you see it, the way I can?
I would ski, ski down a slope,
doing my own stunts in a golden suit.
Backdrop pine trees shining, shining,
glowing, glowing in a copper light.
Through the forest of birthday candles
I would fly. Oh, I would fly.

Kathleen A. Rogers, fifty-three, is a teacher, writer, and actor. She wrote this poem for her sisters-in-law, both of whom have been diagnosed with cancer. "The image of being cast in a part against one's will," she says, "represents the awfulness of facing mortality long before you assumed you would have to deal with it." Both sisters-in-law are cancer survivors.

Recent published work by Rogers includes a short story, "Ironing Pillowcases," which appeared in Calyx, *and a poem, "The Moment before the Improvisation," which will be included in an anthology about musician Glenn Gould.*

Rogers lives with husband Rick Teller in Hull, Massachusetts.

THE GOOD DOCTORS

by Ruthann Robson

It's snowing, of course, as I leave New York,
ice on the highway north.
Call it a second opinion I'm traveling for,
but it's more like salvation.

And if not in Massachusetts, then I'll try Texas,
Tacoma. I hear there's a place in Germany,
a Chi Gong Master in Santa Monica,
a Rife machine, a psychic retreat.

Somewhere there has to be –
Perhaps all my doctors until now
have been impostors. I read a statistic:
there's a one in fifty probability.

And in the famous hospital, haven't I seen
at least a hundred, if I count the radiologists,
the pathologists, the trainees?
All with the same grim prediction for me.

Now in this small office in Boston
with the same pictures of my same body
illuminated by the same brand of light-box,
the prognosis of my universe shifts.

The oncologist and the surgeon
are talking operations and options,
are saying, oh people live years with this,
as if science was as easy as willpower.

And if one looks like an elf
and the other has dandruff,
what I see in their eyes is possibility:
I may not have to die just yet.

*Ruthann Robson, forty-four, was diagnosed with liposarcoma in October
1998. "This poem is one in a series that reflects my journey from a famous
cancer center, where I was treated with chemotherapy and then told my situa-
tion was hopeless, to Dana Farber Cancer Institute in Boston, where I found
other specialists, had a major surgery, and was rediagnosed. I am now doing
well. The experience has inspired me to write numerous poems, which I am
just beginning to submit for publication."*

Robson's collection of poetry, titled Masks *(Leapfrog Press, 1998), was
selected by* Library Journal *as one of the best poetry books of 1999. She also
has authored novels, collections of short fiction, and nonfiction books.*

*Robson lives in New York where she works as a professor of law at the
City University of New York School of Law.*

PROSTATE CANCER AS A SPORTING EVENT

by Ric Masten

castigated by my sister I'm told
"never refer to it again as
'my cancer'"
and "Helpline Harry" says
I'm the captain of the ship
in other words in this house
I hold the channel changer
right now I'm on Channel 9
running the marathon
a race in which it matters not
how quick you came off the blocks
what matters is keeping pace
and possessing a finishing kick
blistering hot

click – over to basketball
not a sport for short people
hell when I was forty
I was already so far behind I decided
there and then that winning the game
is not what's important
what is important
is that I look good losing

click – football is a world of hurt
knocks and hits
and playing through the pain
to a place in the game
where we're five points down
with seconds to go
a "never say die" situation
the old flea flicker – I let the ball fly . . .

click – over to baseball
of late my favorite sport
played on a diamond in a field of grass
bleachers sunshine and always
the possibility of extra innings
theoretically
the contest can last forever
but reality being what reality is
one day the arm will tire
with Sammy Sosa at the plate
on deck . . . Mark McGuire

click – back to the Hail Mary
me streaking down the field
faking out the linebacker
catching the ball
I fall in the end zone
game over – game won
the fans in the stands Irish waking

click – "if you've just tuned in,
it's the top of the tenth
with the score tied at eight all"
the umpire dusts off the plate
"batter up," he shouts
"play ball!"

"POOR DEVIL!"

by Ric Masten

in my early twenties
I went along with Dylan Thomas
boasting that I wanted to go out
not gently but raging
shaking my fist
staring death down

however this daring statement
was somewhat revised
when in my forties I realized
that death does the staring
I do the down

so I began hoping
it would happen to me
like it happened to the sentry
in all those John Wayne
Fort Apache movies
found dead in the morning
face down – an arrow in the back
"poor devil"
the Sergeant always said
"never knew what hit him"

at the time I liked that
the end taking me
completely by surprise
the bravado left in the hands
of a hard-drinking Welshman
still wet behind the ears

older and wiser now
over seventy
and with a terminal disease
the only thing right about
what the Sergeant said
was the "poor devil" part

"poor devil"
never used an opening
to tell loved ones he loved them
never seized the opportunity
to give praise for the sunrise
or drink in a sunset
moment after moment
passing him by
while he marched through his life
staring straight ahead
believing in tomorrow
"poor devil!"

how much fuller
richer and pleasing life becomes
when you are lucky enough
to see the arrow coming

Since 1968, Ric Masten, seventy-one, has made his entire living composing, performing, and publishing poetry. "I have always tried to put a line of language around what I term 'the pain and the puzzlement of life.' Now I have advanced, metastatic, hormone refractory prostate cancer, a literal pain and major puzzlement." Masten keeps his friends and fans up to date on his health status by posting poems, essays, and medical data on his web site, www.ricmasten.com.

Masten has toured extensively, reading his poetry in the United States, Canada, and England. He has thirteen books to his credit. A new book, Words and One-Liners, *is forthcoming (Carmel Publishing Company, 2001).*

Masten lives with his poet-woodcarver wife, Billie Barbara, in the Big Sur Mountains of California.

FINDING GOD AT MONTEFIORE HOSPITAL

by Lorraine Ryan

I remember the rhythm of the dunking:
the mop going into the pail
Juan squeezing the mop
the mop hitting the floor with a whoosh.
A ritual of three steps –
like bells at the consecration
of the Mass at St. Patrick's Cathedral.
Pine and ammonia rose like incense.

With every move, he looked up:
"How's it really going?"
"Did your boy come up today?"
"How is he doing without you at home?"

Sometimes when I couldn't lift my head
off the pillow –
when vomiting and mouth sores
wouldn't let me speak –
the swish of his mop
bestowed the final blessing
of the night.

After Lorraine Ryan, now fifty-four, was diagnosed with acute leukemia, she spent seven weeks in the hospital recovering from an autologous bone marrow transplant. Doctors would stop by only momentarily, "but this sweet man, Juan, was one of the few people who was genuinely interested, who showed he really cared," says Ryan. Twelve years later, Ryan is cancer free. This is her first published poem.

Ryan teaches English and composition to high school students in Goldsboro, North Carolina. She is the mother of a grown son.

The Cancer Poetry Project

IT SEEMS WE CAN LIVE WITH CANCER NOW

by Bonnie Maurer

the three of us with our surgeries
and remissions: Mother's head bare,
Sister's uterus gone and I with only
one breast. Picture us: the American Women Gothic
posed on our porch. The pitchfork in our missing parts.

We enter that living room in the back of our minds.
During quiet conversation, when the lamp shorts out,
we will show no surprise, really. We will pack up the sofa.
What cancer is farming us?

From the picture window, we notice each maple
leaf fall, and the white alyssum, which spreads
from one root, still full of bloom by the drive.

As scientists listen for signals from alien worlds,
we tune our keen ears to stories of others who have lived
clear for twenty years.

THE ANSWER
Stereotactic core biopsy, July 15, 1998

by Bonnie Maurer

Specks of light prove suspicious.
Nurse, surgeon, radiologist . . .
I am a mountain target their fingers climb.
Melon-moon, geologic wonder
of areola, nipple, ancient mesa for his lips,
milk trees and sea of sponge
that shimmies its own earthshake dance,
they see in the X-ray.
My breast in black and white and gray,
they compress against the glass,
numb, probe with the needle,
and pull out, shining like mica,
small as grains of salt,
the cells that hold the secrets of the world,
benign or otherwise,

cells that make me think
of my daughter's question as we swim:
"How did the world begin, Mama?"
and I tell her,
in water, it all began.
Lightning hit the skin of the sea
and I show her the backs of my old hands.
Specks of light danced on the water.
First one cell, then two . . .
then fish of all kinds
and one day a creature climbed out of the water . . .

and I held you to my breast,
milk spout, berry and plum,
and now at my feet,
through the tunnel of my legs, you swim, glistening.

Bonnie Maurer, fifty-one, didn't intend to write poems about cancer. "I woke up and began composing 'The Answer' the morning of my biopsy appointment. I had not written for a while and the experience of waking up practically with a pen in my hand took me by surprise. During my breast cancer, I kept a notebook. I was propelled to a new land, learning a new language."

Six months later, Maurer applied for and won a Creative Renewal Arts Fellowship from the Arts Council of Indianapolis with a proposal to write a poetry manuscript, "The Reconfigured Goddess," about her experiences with breast cancer. Her mother had been diagnosed with lymphoma a month before Maurer's diagnosis, and her sister was diagnosed with cancer a year later. "Makes you wonder," she says.

A poet with three chapbooks and a number of awards to her name, Maurer works as a poet in residence for Young Audiences of Indiana and as a copy editor for the Indianapolis Business Journal. *She lives in Indianapolis with her husband, son, daughter, and cat.*

BI BYE-BYE, BUY

by Mary Milton

A few days before my bilateral mastectomy
a friend cautions
"Don't start buying stuff to compensate"
I blush at his omniscient warning
I have purchased things
a set of bed sheets dusty coral
so blood stains won't show much
and shirts that open in front
one short-sleeved white
bad choice of color but I liked
its spirited portrayal of zebras
galloping through ferns
and gold paint splats
Besides it was on sale
Another long-sleeved shirt
tan and lilac plaid
rayon-cotton blend, soft and comforting
On sale

"Don't start buying stuff to compensate"
What next?
Double scoops of strawberry ice cream?
Vacations to Minneapolis-St. Paul?
Gold caps on my upper lateral incisors?
Stereophonic earphones?
Binoculars?
I picture myself buying on credit
duplicate sports cars in burgundy and cream
a house with twin garrets
I imagine throwing myself on the mercy
of bankruptcy court
Surely the court would show compassion
to a woman who lost both breasts

Or would it?
I'm getting a headache
I think I need new socks

*Mary Milton, sixty-two, wrote "Bi Bye-Bye, Buy" after a friend advised her
not to start buying things to compensate for her upcoming mastectomies. "I
wasn't about to tell him that I'd already started to buy things," Milton says.
"Then I saw the humor in it, so I wrote this poem."*

Milton has had another breast cancer poem published in Art.Rage.Us:
Art and Writing by Women with Breast Cancer *(Chronicle Books, 1998).
A member of Fresh Ink, a local writing group, Milton has had her work
included in a number of journals, including* California Poetry Quarterly
and Bay Area Poets Coalition. *She works as a speech and language therapist
in the Richmond, California, public schools. Milton lives with her dog and
three cats in El Cerrito, California.*

THE CANCER PATIENT TALKS BACK

by Molly Redmond

No.
I don't want to hear about your uncle
and how he lived three years
after being diagnosed.
And I don't want to hear
how many times your cousin threw up
when she had chemo.
Nor how your neighbor's baby
had twelve toes
maybe from radiation.

And I don't want your sounds of pity
simpering about my situation.
Pity separates us and
with one out of three getting cancer now,
pity won't keep you safe.

I have suddenly crossed the boundary line
of the risky circle called cancer.
It has made me public property, like being largely pregnant.
People invade – an assault of connections –
for reasons fair and foul.
Strangers on elevators. Acquaintances.
The medical cadre, too.
Either way,
I am covered with fingerprints, with labels.

Yes.
I will take hugs, help,
plus anger, strength, and love.

But the only person I want to hear about
is your Grandma Ruth,
who was diagnosed at fifty
and died at ninety,
skydiving.

Otherwise,
hold your tongue.

Molly Redmond, fifty-seven, was diagnosed with breast cancer in 1993. She quickly found herself confronted by friends and acquaintances who seemed compelled to share stories about others' cancer experiences – often with dire endings. "I was getting pretty frustrated by it all, and I have since learned that this phenomenon has happened to most cancer survivors," she says. "While I have my guesses about the psychology behind this story sharing, I know now that an effective response is to quickly and nicely interrupt at the very beginning and say something like, 'I need to listen only to stories with happy endings to help me heal.'" Redmond herself has a happy ending, as she is doing well. This is her first published poem.

Redmond lives in St. Paul, Minnesota, with her husband, their teenager, a cheerful golden retriever, and several growing stacks of books she is voraciously devouring.

BECAUSE A WORLD MAY BE CALLED INTO BEING

by Gary Young

Because a world may be called into being, or talked away, the voice inside never quits. I once shamed a boy, called him bed wetter in front of his friends, and the voice kept me up all night, repeating the bitter words. Later, the voice said, cancer, and she's dead. She's dead. You have cancer. This morning the air is sweet with bunchgrass and the smell of horses milling in the corral. It's my birthday. I'm forty-one, and the voice says, you're in Wyoming. I am so happy, and I hear it again, you're in Wyoming.

In 1978, Gary Young, now forty-nine, underwent a radical neck dissection after a level-four malignant melanoma was discovered in his head. "My chances of survival were considered extremely low. I volunteered to participate in a double-blind experiment, but the drug turned out to be ineffective. Nevertheless, to this day, I believe that whatever they injected into me – or perhaps simply my faith in it – contributed to my survival.

"Shortly after, my lover developed ovarian cancer, and within a few months she was dead. With her cancer dovetailing my own, I felt inspired to write my book, Braver Deeds *(Gibbs Smith, 1999), which contained the poem 'Because a world may be called into being.' This poem describes how the voice in our head creates and maintains the world we inhabit. When we have cancer, that internal voice reminds us of the fact incessantly. This is not altogether a bad thing.*

"Five years ago, another melanoma appeared on my leg. I had more surgery, and today, so far as I know, I am disease free. Still, cancer never really leaves; it returns as a voice, a pain, a reminder of the past and an omen of the future. If you're lucky, it becomes a friend."

Young is both an artist and a poet. His print work is represented in many collections, including the Museum of Modern Art and the Getty Center for the Arts. He edits the Greenhouse Review Press *from Santa Cruz, California, where he lives with his wife and two sons.*

A MAN LEARNING WOMEN

by David Zeiger

In the breast clinic
they think he's waiting for his wife.
Then the doctor's nurse calls his name
and he hurries in to strip
and be examined.
The women stare at each other
in disbelief.

In a circle,
a man among women hoisting arms
over mastectomies,
reaching for the edge of their pain.
What haunts him
is the terrible gift of sharing it.
What haunts them
is how he can share it –
their fear strolling the hospital corridor
in lacy peignoirs, holding hands
with their men,
their prayer it will make no difference,
the missing side,
when a lover's hands falter.

In a circle,
nine women and a man reach up
with pulleys over severed flesh,
explore each other's eyes.
Lymph drains bang against their thighs.

His skin stretched and stitched
over rib cage
where pectoral muscle and nipple were,
he remembers cupping and tonguing
a breast.
Tactile tenderness now lost
to these women.

He's heard their soundless moans,
knows the desperate places
behind their eyes,
the quiver of hope and forced smiles
when the social worker enters
to talk prosthesis, and he leaves.

Among the one-half of one percent of men,
reluctant partner
in this circle of wounds,
he's tired of doctors' jests,
their flippant air.
Tired of pills with a woman's portrait
as logo, tired of crossing over
into their grief.

But this shared loss reeking
of bad dreams binds them.
The need to resist the stratagem
of despair.
The will to remake one's self
out of memory.

Male innocence gone, he's learned
to think like a woman.

In this poem, David Zeiger, seventy-nine, recounts his battle with breast cancer at the Sloan-Kettering Cancer Center. His treatment included taking tamoxifen, which is typically prescribed for women, for five years. Zeiger's poetry has appeared in various periodicals and anthologies, and he has been nominated for a Pushcart Poetry Prize. "A Man Learning Women" appears in his self-published chapbook, Life on My Breath *(1995).*

A retired professor of English at the Fashion Institute of Technology, Zeiger lives with his wife in New York City. They have two children and two grandchildren.

LETTERS RECEIVED

by Denise Larrabee

You are in my thoughts
are with you are part of
the "prayer chain" at our
church will say a mass
for you accept all
prayers on your behalf we
will say a rosary for you
tonight lots of people
are calmly, psychically
cheering you on Sunday
will light a candle for
you are in our thoughts
and prayers are being
said for you need all the
health karma there is a
candle lit for you in
front of my Madonna has a
special place for young
women in trouble require
positive and healthy
energy to kiss someone
you love when you get
this letter and make
magic.

Denise Larrabee, forty, was diagnosed with Hodgkin's lymphoma in 1995. "I was declared to be in remission after six months of chemotherapy and radiation treatments," she says. "Both of my sons were born after my cancer experience, which I guess is a testament to my present good health.

"The illness was very isolating. I still sometimes feel a lingering sense of isolation, even as a cancer survivor. I view writing as one way to break through this isolation." Larrabee used lines and phrases from well-wishers' letters to create this poem.

A writer and historian, Larrabee is the author of Anne Hampton Brewster: Nineteenth-Century Author and Social Outlaw *(Library Company of Philadelphia, 1992). Her essays and short stories have appeared in such publications as* Meridian Bound, The Philadelphia Inquirer Magazine, American Writing, *and* Northeast Corridor. *She lives in Philadelphia with her husband and two sons.*

WHEN I INHERIT THE STAR

by Lauren E. Alexanderson

When I inherit the star,
I will pull the plug on these plastic lines
Binding me to a black-and-white hall.
I will paint my room
Until it smells of fresh lilacs,
And I will hang a eucalyptus right
Above your scalpel;
The one that becomes
more sterile with every cut.
I'll water my new plant,
And as the roots soak up life,
The rich soil will spill over onto your
Ceaselessly cold instruments
And give them their first taste of nature.

When I inherit the star,
I will soar toward my midsummer night's dream
I'll let waterfalls swallow me and
Erase your signatures on my neck and arm.
I'll launch my white cotton turban
And let the beams of light meet their mirror,
My head,
Where the shooting stars will dance
And take root in my scalp.
I will have hair brighter than the moon
And long enough to wrap between my toes.

When I inherit the star,
My weight will double.
I'll wear a strapless, silk, pale blue dress.
My curves will put Barbie to shame,
Watching me through green eyes,
As I wrap my shoulders in a taffeta shawl.

Diamond stars woven into my golden mane,
My feet laced into silver Nina sandals.
On my finger a diamond is locked between
Two heart-shaped aquamarines.

Take these needles out of my foot;
You won't find a vein there.
Give me one more night to prove
That I can still be Cinderella
Vånta hår.*
Let me be twenty-one tonight,
I only have one chance to do so.
I promise to return, and when I do,
I will be eleven again.

And you may wrap me in the plastic wires
And walk me down the black-and-white hall
To my room, where my eucalyptus
Is shattered on the sidewalk below,
My ring, my dress, and my shoes locked in a glass
Case, tempting me in my midsummer night's dream
As I sleep among long strands of hair, still
Wrapped between my toes.

*Vånta hår means "wait here" in Swedish.

Lauren E. Alexanderson, seventeen, was diagnosed at age eleven with osteosarcoma, the most common form of bone cancer in children. She received treatment for a year, during which time she served as a Starbright Pioneer for Steven Spielberg and Norman Schwartzkopf's Starbright Pediatric Network, an organization that empowers children with serious illness. Today, she writes poetry to process her feelings concerning her cancer experiences and continuing checkups. "'When I inherit the star' began as a growing-up poem," she says, "but it struck a nerve with me" and became a cancer poem. This is her first published poem.

Alexanderson lives with her parents in Plainfield, New Jersey, where she is a junior in high school.

REMINISCENCE

by Ruth Molly James

The day I finished chemotherapy
they surrounded me with a group hug.
I said, "You have been kind to me.
I will miss you."
They said, "It is good to miss us.
Remember us,
but don't come back."

The day I finished radiation
they cheered and gave me
their autographed certificate.
I said, "You have been gentle and kind.
I will miss you."
They said, "It is good to miss us.
Remember us,
but don't return."

Today I recover.
I remember them.
I sigh. And I smile.
But I don't come back.

Throughout her experience with breast cancer, Ruth Molly James, sixty-seven, kept a journal as assigned by her doctors. When she heard about the Cancer Poetry Project, she wrote a poem based on a journal entry she had written about the medical professionals who had cared for her. "They become such a big part of your life and your healing," James says. "I became very fond of them and realized I wouldn't see them anymore. Mostly, they were young people doing their tough work, so kind, so cheerful, so human." This is her first published poem.

James lives in Grant City, Minnesota, with husband Alan. A retired nurse, she has three sons, three grandsons, and a pet llama named Gazpachoo.

THE SPY

by Marlene Rosen Fine

In the photographs the doctors hold
I see the spy.
They have deciphered your code.
They will track you down.
Traitorous cell.
You have set up quarters in my breast.
You send your signals beneath my skin
making small revolutions
in my underground city.

But the generals are conferring
at the foot of my bed.
Cold and brutal,
they will have no pity.
They will never rest
till they cut you out.
They are the forces
pharmaceutical.

THE BREAST

by Marlene Rosen Fine

Hunting close to the bone
the surgeon moves
from clues
to the final
routing
and then the skin is sewn

His fingers take a part of me
so I can keep my life

All night long
I sing of pain
O he marvels that I sing so loud
and I, that I can sing at all

He is part of the silent wall
and I am of the shouting

This then I give to you
my lover
my forever cockeyed chest

This then I give to you my child
the stories of before
when two pokey softenings rode me

Little daughter, you dream
I grow another breast
and cry to wake me

But listen, as we whisper in the fuzzy night,
know that I've two of everything
I'll ever need again

Spare parts are to discover
what I can do without

Marlene Rosen Fine, now sixty, was twenty-eight when she found a lump in her breast while breastfeeding her two-month-old daughter. "My obstetrician/gynecologist was unbelieving," Fine says. She and husband Michael consulted Dr. Hugh Auchincloss, a specialist and surgeon, who recommended that a tissue sample be examined. He diagnosed breast cancer and recommended a radical mastectomy, which was immediately performed. Seven months later, Fine needed radiation, then an oophorectomy to stop the supply of hormones to this hormone-dependent cancer, which had flourished during her "otherwise healthy, joyous nine months of pregnancy."

"My conclusion," Fine says, "as I watch my grown-up son and daughter, as I love my husband more than ever and feel his love for me, as I work, write, and give my best deeds to my family and friends, is that Dr. Auchincloss saved my life."

Fine's award-winning work has been published in numerous literary magazines, and she expects to publish her collected poetry. She has read her poetry in bars, coffeehouses, bookstores, and museums all over New York City. She lives and works with her husband, the publisher of MJF Books.

ONCOLOGY IN ADVENT

by Bonnie Thurston

Theologians say
the Cosmic Christ
is operative in all things.
I'm waiting to see it.

Where are You
in the oncology waiting room
with its window on a gray day,
in a has-been neighborhood?

Where are You, then,
when they wheel in
the bald young woman
obviously too sick to be here?

Where are You
when diseases maim and kill
not quickly and cleanly,
but with messy tendentiousness?

How am I to see you here
unless, perhaps, as Emmanuel,
a fellow sufferer,
bald and trembling.

Bonnie Thurston, forty-eight, was diagnosed with cancer in December 1998. She is sure she will be healed, if not cured. "I wrote this poem after seeing a woman in the oncology waiting room who was obviously much sicker than I was. I am a Christian pastor and a seminary professor, and, looking at her, I 'saw Jesus,' or at least was reminded again that we do not have a God who hides out in heaven when we suffer. God has taken on human flesh and shares our suffering. I also know this as the widow of a husband who died of pancreatic cancer."

Thurston's poetry has been published in magazines and journals in the United States and United Kingdom. She is the author of numerous articles and books in the field of biblical studies and spirituality, the most recent of which are To Everything a Season: A Spirituality of Time *(Crossroad, 1999) and* Fruit of the Spirit, Growth of the Heart *(Liturgical Press, 2000).*

Thurston, a New Testament professor at Pittsburgh Theological Seminary, lives in Wheeling, West Virginia.

IMPOTENCE

by Harvey Overton

The Marlboro Man who rides an office chair
and cheers on Sunday for the NFL,
who loves his wife, his kids, his evening beer,
against the odds has lost his bet. He tells
himself what he denies – no doctor's trick
can help, no potion, not a patient wife.
In fairness every man's climacteric
should fade in with the night; the surgeon's knife
brought his, and now he wakes at midnight when
he wonders what is meant by love. Because
he learned his father's myth that men are men
for what's between their legs,
he never paused
to separate his loving from his sex.
It hurts more than you think. He's fifty-six.

*Harvey Overton, seventy-nine, says he is doing well – waiting and watching,
but feeling optimistic after his bout with prostate cancer four years ago. "Since
several of my friends have died of or are now burdened with this disease, and
because so few men have written about it, I thought that the subject should be
addressed in poetry," he says. His fourteen poems on the subject, written in a
number of voices, are included in his chapbook,* How We Measure Fourteen
and Other Poems *(The Hidkey Press, 1998).*

*Overton taught for more than thirty years in the humanities department
of Western Michigan University. Since retirement, he has been able to focus
on his poetry and has had three collections published by small presses. He lives
with wife Jean in Chicago.*

The Cancer Poetry Project

VARIATIONS ON MY ROOM IN THE
BONE MARROW UNIT: IN THE ROOM OF COWS

by Julie Moulds

Marc Chagall's peasant is milking a red Jersey cow
incessantly, letting flow a river of cream across
a muddy floor. Here is a peaceable kingdom of cows,
Danish next to Holstein next to Swiss. The bulls have had
their testosterone lowered with medication and now lie meekly
with the skittish rest of the herd. They no longer bang
their steaming heads against the barn wall when I enter.
The hospital nurse in a cow uniform keeps trying
to tie us into blue gowns, taking advantage of our new
docility. This room is as large as a field but is still
a room. It opens with a double-hinged hospital door.
I sit in a corner, at a drugstore soda counter, having
a coffee milkshake. After blessing the cow and coffee bean,
I lace the shake with my latest prescription, a syrup
for mouth sores, a Christmas gift from my pharmacist.
A Holstein serves me, like Elsie in her apron, and a Longhorn
tries to pick me up, but he is easy to resist.
I prefer men, though I know there are other options.
Chagall says hello, but isn't interested in females without hair,
however jewel blue and red my scarf is. After my shake,
I sleep on clean heaped straw. A nurse hooks me up
to an IV of chocolate milk, vitamin fortified.
She gossips of great bulls she has known, steamy nights
of alfalfa and Merlot with a Beefmaster in Vegas;
and that recent *ménage à trois* with the Angus brothers
in a pole barn. I make up some travels to India, and a tryst
with a Brahman bull as she checks all my lines:
IV tubes flowing in, and Foley catheters running out.

ONE HUNDRED AND TEN DAYS

by Julie Moulds

Under this roof of rectangular things: the motorized bed;
electrical outlets; metallic IV machines, clicking
and humming – the only things oddly shaped are the people
in the angled-up beds and the round hanging bags
of chemotherapy. The bed-riding person must push
a red button for a nurse to come: *Nurse, I can't breathe. Nurse, I have
anger. Nurse, let me die.* In the bathroom,
where urine is carefully measured, a beaded string
can be pulled for help, the spaced plastic beads like a cheap
childhood rosary. There'd be surprisingly little to watch
from the sky. Nurses run in and out. Patients are patient
or not. Doctors are caring or not (even their hellos
cost seventy-five dollars). The hallways are oval,
like a high school track. The nurses go on rounds
and wake you with anti-fungal mouth medications,
racks of test tubes and blood-pressure cuffs.
The thermometer beeps when it decides your temperature.
You never get used to the way veins constrict
during pressure checks; never get used to the endless line
of needles: blood oxygen pricks on hands, IVs inserted
into arm and chest, blood drawings inside elbows,
huge bone marrow needles in the hip bones.
(You say *next time you stick that stake in me,
damn well make sure I'm unconscious.*) You might as well
be an appliance plugged to the wall, each five days
of chemotherapy. Move, and alarms go off. Unplug yourself;
alarms go off. The chemotherapy drips, clicks, hums
into veins. The anti-nauseas fog you up.
You flip the TV channels: try to focus on *Star Trek,
Barney, Regis and Kathy Lee,* then use your hospital tray
for a desk, writing valentines, wedding thank-yous,
Christmas cards, on drugs. You recopy your address book,
grade your students' class work, on drugs. Everyone gets an A.

Thirty days in the bone marrow unit and you never leave
the room. You think of Madeline who studied the crack
in her hospital ceiling, the one that looked like a rabbit;
play with the blue paper mask the cleaning girl gives you
when she comes in. You turn the mask into a tent, a bedpan,
a bow tie, a bonnet, a moth, a kidney. You start to order
plain mashed potatoes and cream of wheat for meals.
You could easily starve yourself; put a photo of your family
by the bed. Once a day, the nurse unhooks you
from the IV to shower, covers your chest with plastic wrap,
then leaves. You always take longer than you need
in the water – stay under its pulse; rinse off the strange
chemical smells you emit. And after you step out,
drying slowly, and peeling the plastic from under arm
and over nipple, you try to cover the hospital's smell
with baby powder, change to a fresh blue gown.
You could walk to the bed, call the nurse, say, *I'm ready
to be re-hooked now,* but never do. There are whole minutes
when you keep the door closed and walk to every corner
of the room, not connected to anything.

---

*Julie Moulds, thirty-eight, wrote these poems after her initial treatment for
non-Hodgkin's lymphoma and a subsequent bone marrow transplant. "I was
journaling throughout the process, working so hard to be positive for my
health. Then, after I'd been in remission, negative thoughts started coming
out in my poetry." While there is some humor in her poems, Moulds notes
that a lot of cancer humor is black humor.*

*"Variations on My Room in the Bone Marrow Unit: In the Room of Cows"
is one of several "room" poems she has written, where anything can happen except
she cannot leave the room. "One Hundred and Ten Days" refers to the number
of days she spent in the hospital. Both selections were first published in* The
Woman with a Cubed Head *(New Issues Poetry Press, 1998). While Moulds is
no longer in remission – indolent (or lazy) tumors with no symptoms have been
found – she is looking forward to beginning a promising new treatment soon.*

*Moulds lives with husband John Rybicki (see his poems on pages 65 and
66) in Delton, Michigan, where she teaches creative writing and works at a
children's bookstore.*

MIDNIGHT IN THE PRETTY LITTLE HOUSE

by Greg Keith

The radiation oncologist won't call back now until tomorrow.
The lump in my cheek feels the same size as this morning,
time passes no faster. Mortal fear opens a space in the body,
an empty center near the belly but larger than a belly, a suction
felt in arms and legs grown somehow hollow. I am that and not that.

Neither the feeling nor the thing felt, I seem. Mere ideas
churn the seeming. If this is cancer back so soon
so smack dab in the middle of the radiated field, then
it's time to put my goodbye practice to good use now.

I carry the newspaper bundle to the curb for predawn pickup, a few
board feet they won't have to cut again. Jupiter bright toward the ecliptic,
ongoing. In the driveway the idea cannot be resisted: The sky and the house
will survive me, certainly the plumbing, the ginger in the flower bed,
the brass hinges, perhaps the light bulbs.

Inside my fingers, sometimes called my extremities, the open feeling
goes on quivering slightly while they hover over the keyboard.

Greg Keith died in June 1998, at age fifty-two, after battling squamous cell carcinoma for over a year. This poem, which was included in his chapbook titled Life Near 310 Kelvin *(SLG Books, 1998), was submitted by wife Susan Borton Keith, who 8had married him just eighty days before his death.*

Keith kept a journal on his web site, which friends and relatives would check every day. "I wouldn't have ordered cancer off the menu," he wrote. "But we all get to die, and most of us get to suffer. It's not that I'm happy all the bone is gone. I don't enjoy radiation or spikes of anxiety, but there are moments when a kind of glee fills me about how real it all is, how the little connections that get made or verified between me and other people fill up with such joy now."

Keith's poems were published in such journals as Chelsea, Kalliope, *and* The Literary Review. *Surviving him are his wife and two daughters.*

FIRST SUMMER

by Joan Annsfire

that first summer after recovery,
the Oregon landscape
was a work of art, vivid and deep
slices of cloudless blue opened
into evergreen valleys
bounded by a massive,
all-encompassing
horizon.

we swam naked
in water clear, fast and cold,
dove and darted under electrified sunshine,
yellow and pink limbs moving
strong and hard against the current
high on the exhilaration of narrow escape
and second chances.

I was still feeling fragile, uncertain,
the hollow place on my thigh etched
with a deep purple scar,
the mark of one who has shed her skin
and stepped out, transformed
into this undeterrable rush
of water.

round, flat leaves, half-lit by sunlight,
fluttered in the late afternoon breeze.
the western wind carried notes of a tune
drifting in from somewhere
far away.

later that night in the cabin
other songs came to me.
shrill crickets called down the August twilight
as it faded into September
and the last beads were added
to the string of long, warm,
summer evenings.

melody, melodies,
melancholy, melodrama,
melanoma, melanoma,
how can a word so like music
imply the possibility of the end of this fierce beauty?
syllables whose sound alone conjures up
images of villas on the Mediterranean
and flamboyant Spanish dances.

yet, all that summer
that single word bounced around inside my head
until the leaves themselves whispered it
and it was tossed from rock to rock
by the river.

so when you said that you could appreciate
being here compared to being at work
but didn't want to contemplate
being here in contrast to not being at all,
I couldn't understand your desire to filter out
this intense sensation of joy.

if only I could place it within you,
you would marvel at the dance of light and shadow
on the water's moving surface,
rejoice in the rampaging masterpiece
of an unconquerable river
beneath a gradually
darkening
sky.

The Cancer Poetry Project

Joan Annsfire, fifty, is a poet, writer, and librarian for the James Hormel Gay and Lesbian Center in San Francisco. She lives in Berkeley, California. Diagnosed with a level-four malignant melanoma in 1991, Annsfire is now cancer free and in excellent health.

" 'First Summer' was written the summer after my cancer surgery, while on a trip to Oregon with my partner," she says. "I was high on living and doing a tremendous amount of writing. I felt that I'd been given a second chance to live the life I had aspired to as a young person, and the feelings were intense. This poem was the first in a series of writings about cancer, which included pieces about my mother's death from ovarian cancer when she was forty-eight and I was twenty-two. The years since my cancer experience have been so much more precious than I ever would have imagined. It seems like a new door opens every day."

Recently, Annsfire has been volunteering as poetry editor for the Sinister Wisdom Collective. Her work has appeared in such journals as Women's Cancer Resource Center Newsletter, Mediphors, Evergreen Chronicles, *and* Bridges.

WHEN I HAD CANCER I THOUGHT

by Mark Sheffield Brown

When I had cancer I thought
that the tomatoes I cut at work
were red, frosty hearts –
fleshy and giving
when the knife came,

that the white, plastic arch
of the CT machine
was a smooth, bone mouth
devouring me,

that the pixel image
of my pelvis bone
from the underside
was an ancient Egyptian priest
holding open his arms,
his hanging robes.

I guess that just goes to show
how fragile we are,
how scared,
how sacred.

Mark Sheffield Brown, twenty-seven, was employed at a local pizza and sub shop during his undergraduate years when he was diagnosed with testicular cancer. "My wife and I went to the urologist in the afternoon, where I was told I had a tumor. From there I went almost directly to work, where everything had a disjointed, surreal feeling to it. Slicing tomatoes as part of my prep work, I watched the knife pass through their skins, saw the thin, red juice leak out . . . it was kind of disturbing and fascinating at the same time. Later I had the experience of getting a CT scan. These powerful images stuck with me and eventually came out in the poem."

Today, Brown says he is "healthy as can be, with plenty of energy and not a cancer cell in sight." He lives with wife Suzanne in Boise, Idaho, where he is a teaching assistant and MFA student at Boise State University. His poetry has appeared in such journals as Ethos *and* The New Zoo Poetry Review.

THERE'S NOT A BOOK ON HOW TO DO THIS

by Sharon Doyle

There's not a book on how to do this,
but there is an emphasis on composition.

The trucks that slug by under our window
hold trombones, mirrors, dictionaries.
It's not my fault they invade
the calm of the trees like cancer. I

don't have cancer anymore. After nine
months my hair grew again and I
was sure I had given birth to
myself. "This helps to learn some about

patience," they said, and I relaxed
for days. But this night the
moon was exactly half, and porous,
and grand. I rarely remember the

uterus I don't have. One of my sons said,
"You were done with it anyway, right, Mom?"
I guessed so. The trees still carry on with
magpies; my husband bought me a clock with

birdsongs; I planted a bush of scarlet
bells for tempting hummingbirds;
my daughters gave me a miniature rose when
I left the hospital.

Finally this morning I finished
sketching my garden for fall.
I left vacant fourteen
trellis lightscapes for
balloons.

At first, her cancer diagnosis seemed like a death sentence, says Sharon Doyle, fifty-seven. "But ever since then, the people I love, my doctors, and other cancer patients have taught me how to live with hope, and how to get and use the knowledge that can cure me. In fact, the entire experience has made my life richer." This poem tries to say that "a person diagnosed with cancer has to figure out what to do about it."

Doyle taught English in junior high and college for several years before leaving teaching to raise her five children. Today she spends a great deal of time with her seven grandchildren, and she writes extensively. Doyle lives with husband James in Fort Collins, Colorado. His poem, "The cancerous cell," is found on page 102.

HOW TO STAY ALIVE

by Judith Strasser

Trash your cigarettes. Shun restaurants and bars
that traffic in secondhand smoke. Eat organic
and low on the food chain. Steam vegetables;
don't grill meat. Just say "no" to marijuana, Jack
Daniels, and cocaine. Stay home: do not rent cars
at Miami's airport, or ride the New York subways,
or dig potshards in the Negev after massacres
in Hebron. Don't drive vans older than you are
to places you've never been. Always buckle your
seat belt. Have someone else strip the asbestos
from your furnace and heating pipes. Test for radon
in the basement, lead in the drinking water, cracks
in the microwave shield. Avoid electric blankets.
Use condoms, or don't have sex. Walk to work.
Remember your sunblock. Don't go jogging after dark.
Keep off the neighbors' grass after they've sprayed
the yard. Wear a helmet when you bike. Take
a buddy to the lake. Don't lie about your weight
to the man who adjusts your skis. Lower stress
with yoga; divorce your husband if you must. Cross
your fingers, say "Star Bright" to Venus, avoid
black cats, spit three times over your shoulder
on your thirteenth annual visit to the oncologist.

Judith Strasser, fifty-six, wrote "How to Stay Alive" thirteen years after her diagnosis and treatment for Hodgkin's disease, while "fighting the anxiety that always comes in the weeks before my annual oncology checkup," she says. "I had other reasons for anxiety, too. My oldest son, who had just started college, was driving around in a twenty-two-year-old rusted-out Dodge van, and my father had gone on an archeological dig in the Negev around the time of the Gulf War. I bundled all my anxieties into one poem and tried to put them outside of me." This poem first appeared in Prairie Schooner.

Strasser lives in Madison, Wisconsin, where she is an interviewer for the nationally syndicated public radio program, To the Best of Our Knowledge, *and for "Out Loud," the audio feature of the Poets and Writers web site. She has two grown sons: Jed Ela, a conceptual artist who lives in Brooklyn, New York, and Nate Ela, who is in the Peace Corps teaching English in Mozambique.*

RECONSTRUCTION

by Lisa Katz

You say I should rebuild
with a sack of plastic, or
one part of the body
replaces another.

A woman might love
a man without a leg.
They can have children.
And men whose legs
don't work
make children
with women who climb on.
Sometimes a child disappears
like a lost limb.

Couldn't we have
a different aesthetic,
asymmetrical,
Japanese,
because of the war,
because islands get invaded.

Couldn't we
admire the ruined, the torn, the perfect
error, because the weaver
skips a row
for the sake of humility,
because your love
needs a few stitches?

See the scar,
the flat plain on my chest.
Connect the dots.
Do you have the courage?
You won't get many chances
to look at an absence straight on,
to look at something missing,
missing in such a prominent way.

"I didn't choose the theme of this poem; it chose me after I had a mastectomy and chemotherapy three years ago," says Lisa Katz, fifty-one. "I wanted to look at the process from an ironic distance, to feel that I had some control over my life. And I wanted to give solace and a feeling of control to other women undergoing this terrifying and yet humanizing disease. I say 'humanizing' because the loss of a beloved part of the body can teach us that we are more than merely body – and this is a lesson that we can share with others, too. We begin to look more sharply at the people around us, and to demand more of life. It's a gift."

"Reconstruction" is one of a series of poems by Katz called "Breast Art," which was translated into Hebrew and published in an Israeli literary magazine. This poem also won honorable mention in the Pablo Neruda Poetry Competition and was published in Nimrod. *Another poem by Katz was read at a meeting of the Israeli Knesset Committee on the Status of Women. Her translations of ten Israeli poets appear in* Poetry International #4.

Katz lives with her husband and two children in Jerusalem, Israel, where she translates from Hebrew into English and teaches in the English department of Hebrew University.

DIAMONDS

by Marcia Renée Goodman

After you've had cancer, hope becomes your job.
Each day you have to do it nine to five at least
to support yourself and those who love you.

You pretend that you're not worried when you catch a cold,
say to your husband, "Even after cancer there are colds."
And if some lab test gives ambiguous results,
you tell your parents, "It's nothing, nothing."

You convince yourself to live each day to the fullest,
following out the cliché of your own experience.
You hide your fear from your young children and
tell your friends one truth,
which is that the prognosis is relatively good.
The other you usually don't say.

But sometimes the heaviness of hope gets to you
and what you need most is to feel the purity of fear,
to let it burn out the details of your day-to-day life,
to let it escape for a while its crystalline cave.
For the diamonds of that cave glow, too.
Its walls vibrate power.
You live also in this underworld,
you now let yourself know,
here with fear and with a loss
that cannot be compensated.

You know this is a private underworld
and that to talk of it too much might destroy something,
but sometimes hope's burden is too much,
and what you crave more than some sign of perpetual life
is the clarity to say things as they really are.

Marcia Renée Goodman, forty-six, was diagnosed with ovarian cancer in October 1998. She experienced three six-month rounds of chemotherapy, finishing in January 2000. A published poet and teacher of writing and literature at Diablo Valley College, she says, "I started to write about cancer the night I got back from the hospital after my surgery. I awoke frightened of dying. I told myself I had to write, and so I lifted myself up enough to grab the notebook next to my bed, and I wrote about the dream that had awakened me. By writing it down I returned to myself, to the part of me that feels most alive when putting words to paper. Except in e-mails, I didn't write poetry again for a few months. Then, for a while, my writing was pretty sporadic because I felt so ill from the chemo. I know I'm better because I'm writing a lot again, and it feels like such a gift."

Goodman lives in Berkeley, California, and credits her powerful community of friends, her parents, and her family – husband, daughter, son, and two stepsons – with getting her through her cancer experience.

BAY BRIDGE/ROSH CHODESH

by Dori Ehrlich

This moon has almost caused wrecks on the bridge.
A blueblack pancake sliced up by Christmas cables.
this moon needs a Caltrans sign.

My chicken bone leg is bent
so I dare to slide my shoe off
while doing 65 over this nighttime tightrope.

When I tell the mechanic the door handle
dropped on this bridge
he rattles off the list
of car parts that have joggled to this same tragic destiny.

I imagine we all desert parts
flying over an unbridling bridge.
My lane changing
testimony to believing in what cannot be seen
testimony to beautiful catastrophe.

I fling all this off on the bridge:
I kiss tumors goodbye
I shake loose my dented parts
that are dangling off anyway
and, like a muffler.
I bang out old life.
it is left spinning in the street
behind me.

　　　　　　　The Cancer Poetry Project

"I was diagnosed with thyroid cancer when I was twenty-one, which rattled and banged my universe and made me start writing poetry," says Dori Ehrlich, now twenty-four. "'Bay Bridge/Rosh Chodesh' was inspired by the Jewish ritual of the new moon. It is a celebration of my being free of cancer."

Ehrlich teaches at Children's After School Arts, Rooftop Alternative School in San Francisco, California.

HOW WILL DEATH ARRIVE?

by Mildred Erickson Buzenberg

Oh, how will death arrive?
As soft and smooth as silk,
Coaxing my soul to follow
On that short sweet walk?

Or will death arrive like thunder,
Like a frightening storm at sea,
Roaring, raving and angry,
Grabbing my soul from me?

Will death be mother's hand
Smoothing o'er my brow?
Or is it fierce and frightening,
Like lions on the prowl?

Oh, how will death arrive?
As thunder during rain?
Or might I look on death
As a friend to end my pain?

Mildred Erickson Buzenberg died from bone cancer on Christmas Day 1998 at age eighty-two, after a long remission from breast cancer diagnosed in the 1980s.

"Her illness opened a doorway to her creative nature," says son Bill. "Words crowded her head, persisting until she wrote them down. As she fought the cancer, she found that expressing her experiences in words brought soul-enriching satisfaction." Buzenberg wrote enough material for a short book of poetry, published by her family and given to her on her eightieth birthday. In her last years, she became an accomplished writer of poetry, essays, short stories, and family history.

Buzenberg grew up in Waseca, Minnesota, pursued a business major at Michigan State University, and rose to the rank of assistant dean of Kansas State University's College of Business. She and husband Bob raised four children.

The Cancer Poetry Project

POEMS BY SPOUSES, PARTNERS, AND LOVERS

JULIE ANN IN THE BONE MARROW UNIT, ZION, ILLINOIS

by John Rybicki

Ah, Dame, I don't know how else to love you
so I just start juggling. I'm on the street

three floors below your hospital window,
lofting fish or birds that graze against my hands

and fly off; juggling cancer cells and carnations,
slipping in the bowling pin

we snuck out of that alley in Maine. Then I'm juggling
freight trains, and angels, and elephants,

dropping them all. I don't care. So long as you
can stand near your high window and laugh,

so long as you stand near your hospital bed
clapping your hands.

OUTSIDE THE BONE MARROW UNIT

by John Rybicki

It has been over a year since Julie waved
aside the wheelchair and walked in her own bright bones

out of that sterilized chamber: the butterfly
doors swung open and she stepped into air

that two weeks earlier could have killed her.
I'm worried that thinking about cancer,

writing about cancer, will start cancer
growing again inside her. Where in that sweet void,

where in the wide heavens,
could it be hiding?

I stand on my toes and kiss one of my angels,
and in that kiss beg her

to take a stiff broom to this talk:
sweep the cancer back across the heavens;

please don't miss one crumb of it. Sweep
the cancer back into its black box of oblivion.

"What moved me to write these poems was an abundance of grief," says John Rybicki, whose wife continues to experience non-Hodgkin's lymphoma. "On the page anything is possible, for when we speak with authority, with honesty and audacity and heart, we in many ways reclaim one fistful of God's own fire and drag it down to this world and hurl it across the skin of the page. Julie has crowned my life, and so I insist, I grab God by the scruff of the neck and insist He allow me to exceed myself, to put the power he planted in me to some good use on my gal's behalf – and out of me springs the holiness of poetry."

Rybicki lives with wife Julie Moulds (her poems can be found on pages 43 and 44) in Delton, Michigan. He teaches creative writing at Interlochen Center for the Arts and to inner-city children in Detroit. His first book of poems, Traveling at High Speeds, *was published in 1996 by New Issues Poetry Press.*

DIAGNOSIS

by Natalie Olsen

When the "C" word had been spoken
and we knew for sure,
he wanted things in order.
Tiller blades sharpened,
fence posts checked,
the garden planted.
Things done.

I would have filled today
with friends and food and wine
and reassurances
that everything will be okay.

He tills long, parallel rows of dirt,
our daughter mows.
I spread out crablike strawberry roots,
then rake, and furiously
poke down seeds
wherever I choose,
mixing bachelor buttons, beans and sweet white corn
with marigolds, carrots and thyme.

"I was angry. I didn't want everything to be orderly. I kept thinking, what does it matter?" says Natalie Olsen, sixty-one, regarding this poem about husband Earl's prostate cancer diagnosis nine years ago. Today he is doing well and they both lead active lifestyles, camping and rock climbing.

Olsen's poetry has appeared in a number of journals and on buses in the Seattle area as part of the Poetry Bus Project. A freelance humor writer and fiber artist who creates woven art on commission, Olsen lives with her husband, son Brent, and daughter Krista, in Redmond, Washington, where up until recently she also raised sheep.

The Cancer Poetry Project

GUINEA PIG

by Julie Cadwallader-Staub

As if your cancer weren't enough,
The guinea pig is dying.
The kids brought him to me
Wrapped in a bath towel
Do something, Mom.
Save his life.

I'm a good mom.
I took time from work.
I drove him to the vet.
I paid $77 for his antibiotics.

Now, after the kids rush off to school,
You and I sit on the bed.
I hold the guinea pig (since he bites).
You fill the syringe (since you've had lots of practice).
We administer the foul-smelling medicine
To this black-and-white repository of our children's great love,
Hoping the little fellow will live,
Admitting to each other
If he doesn't
It'll be good practice.

THIS MONTH

by Julie Cadwallader-Staub

I forgot to pay the mortgage
This month.
But I got you to the hospital in time
Every time,
And I made sure you took your medications –
Morphine, Compazine, Atavan, Benadryl, Levoflox, Imodium –
At the right time
Every time.
And I finished the school year
With all three kids –
Homework, projects, concerts, field trips, award ceremonies.
And I kept up
With my own job.
We got through the first phase of this transplant
And another month of wild family life
Pretty well
This month.

So I called the mortgage company
To explain
Why I forgot to pay the mortgage.
I waded through
voice messaging options.
There wasn't one that said
"If you have a reasonable explanation for
Forgetting to pay the mortgage, press 2."
So while I listened again,
Trying to figure out which option might result in a human being,
I checked your temperature.
It was over 101.
I had to hang up,
Call the doctor,

Take you to the hospital.
And forget
That I forgot
To pay the mortgage
This month.

Julie Cadwallader-Staub, forty-four, finds that writing poetry "cuts to the chase" of the cancer experience. "Writing has enormous therapeutic value," says Julie, who had written poetry for a long time as a hobby. But once husband Warren was diagnosed with advanced multiple myeloma (bone marrow cancer), "poetry became an incredibly powerful vehicle for expressing what was going on in our lives. Since then, Warren has experienced two stem cell transplants and numerous chemotherapy treatments, complications, and recoveries. Through it all, poetry has allowed me to touch the deep river of pain within me." Warren, too, has found his wife's poetry beneficial. "She has helped me get through this, because of her poetry," he says. "Her poetry is rich, rich stuff." These are her first published poems.

Cadwallader-Staub works for the Vermont Community Foundation. She lives with her husband and their three children in South Burlington, Vermont.

SLOW DANCING AT THE MED-INN

by F. Richard Thomas

It's the night before your mastectomies.

I'm sitting on the end of the bed.
(We got the faded-orange-curtain-40-watt-lightbulb-
green-chenille-bedspread room.)

From the shower,
you suddenly loom over me,
smelling of peppermint soap and wet leaves
around the lake in the fall.

Holding a breast in each hand,
as if restraining the flight of doves,
you press them to my face and erupt into tears.

I touch my lips to one, then the other,
falter at the scent of my self –
the joyful signature of my fingers and hands.

I pull your body hard to mine,
as if to hurt will help to heal.

The room fades in and out like a bad radio.
The baseboard heater tick tick ticks.

Outside, the helicopter walloping on the roof
lowers a burned child,
stars explode across the night,
volcanoes rise from the ocean floor,
wobble the earth on its axis.

Except for our breathing,
we dare not move.

F. Richard Thomas, sixty, writes poetry about cancer "because it so directly forces us to confront our own mortality," he says. "Cancer releases emotions and fears that we are normally capable of repressing or escaping. Once these have surfaced and are faced head-on, intense feelings of love and joy emerge – which are also feelings that we too often repress." "Slow Dancing at the Med-Inn" was first published in Death at Camp Pahoka *(Michigan State University Press, 2000).*

Thomas' wife, Sharon, has found many lumps in her breasts over the years. All were benign until 1998, when malignant tumors appeared in both breasts simultaneously. Today, Sharon is cancer free.

Richard and Sharon both teach in the Department of American Thought and Language at Michigan State University in East Lansing. Severn and Caerllion, their son and daughter, own and manage the Red Mountain Cafe in Las Cruces, New Mexico.

CHORES

by Perie Longo

Tomorrow will he be stronger?
Tonight will his fever rise again like the tide
beaching him in the ocean of himself?
Tomorrow will I have the energy to wash away
what his body casts off, the energy to hope
when his eyes wander outside to meet
the generosity of tree and sky?

My friend writes I should look
at the moon and stars each night. She means
to offer me strength, but how do we continue?

Tonight the cicada is too loud.
How can it hold one note that long
without taking a breath?

How can I hold our lives alone like this,
him over in his chair gathering himself
while I stir the pot, get this and that,
one eye looking into the dark,
the other on the stove. I step outside
to cut a rose for him.

The cicada begins to sing again.

Perie Longo, sixty, has written a number of poems about her husband's battle with cancer, and she "continues to learn the blessings of life through his illness," she says. "I write to cope, or when a first line comes and I need to follow it through to see what the poem has to tell me."

Longo's poetry has been published in such journals as The Prairie Schooner, Rattle, *and* Studia Mystica. *She also has two collections,* The Privacy of Wind *(1997) and* Milking the Earth *(1986), both published by John Daniel and Company.*

Longo, a psychotherapist in private practice, serves as a staff member of the national Santa Barbara Writers' Conference and the California Poets in the Schools, and is on the board of the National Association of Poetry Therapy. She lives with her family in Santa Barbara, California.

A WALK AT DUSK

by Jere Truer

In mid-August in Minnesota,
dusk falls in clay-colored particles
on tree boughs, on rooftops,
across fields and yards,
bearing the world downward
into sweet melancholy.
The retiring sun's wan smile
bids us release, permission
to let it all go,
every last bit,
of what was unrequited this day,
this year, this life.
So it is that when you and I
walk each evening near the creek
past the dozing houses near home,
old grudges slough off me,
like the clay dust, and are licked up
by the paths of the hungry earth
since death came to live with us.

Jere Truer, forty-eight, has written poetry since his twenties. But when his wife was diagnosed with breast cancer in 1998, he made writing a poem a nightly assignment. "Nighttime was the hardest, feeling all the anxiety," he says. "So I turned to poetry to calm myself. Our walks, too, through our neighborhood near Lake Nokomis, were meant to calm us." Wife Tamara has been cancer free for two-and-a-half years.

Truer, who works as a psychotherapist in private practice in Minneapolis, has had his poetry published in Sidewalks, Kourou, Artword Quarterly, *and other literary journals. He and his wife have a daughter, Kate, who attends Macalester College in St. Paul, Minnesota.*

NUMB

by Florence Weinberger

It is hard to give up after months of making lists,
phoning doctors, fighting entropy. But when the end comes,
a bending takes over, empties the blood of opposition
and with a gentle skill, injects a blessed numbness.
I know the air around me thinned when he stopped breathing,
and, though I did not faint, I could not stand
to stay and watch his dank, soiled clothes removed, his body
turned and washed and shrouded.
Someone led me out and someone sat me down
and someone held me. I heard a sound leave my mouth,
unearthly, unfamiliar. I uttered it only once.
A few days later I dress carefully, as if the habit instilled in a woman
who dresses for public appearances is as much a scar
as a vaccination is. I let others take care of the particulars.
Perhaps this surrender foreshadows my own old age
when I have raged to exhaustion and finally have to go. For now,
the numbness wears off. I drive to the market, cook my own food,
take scant note of desire
with no one else to consider or contradict my choices.
Something in me will never recover. Something in me will go on.

---

*"I was so fortunate to have poetry as an outlet," says Florence Weinberger,
speaking of husband Ted, his diagnosis of metastatic melanoma, and his
death in 1998. "I wrote this particular poem out of anguish and frustration.
My ability to express myself in poetry during this trying time was of enormous help to me."*

*Poems by Weinberger have been published in many literary journals. She
has two chapbooks,* The Invisible Telling Its Shape *(Fithian Press, 1997)
and* Breathing Like a Jew *(Chicory Blue, 1997).*

*Weinberger lives in Encino, California, where she dotes on her four
grandchildren. She is the mother of two daughters.*

ABSENCE OF PLACE

by Rev. Charles Brackbill

I was on automatic. Going for the paper. Going
to bed. Taking out the garbage. One foot in front,
etc. Now chatting as if nothing had happened,
next crying in the shower.

My reputation for rational moves, out the window.
Kübler-Ross had words for this mess. A lot of good it
did me. I, who many times warned the bereaved not
to make any big decisions, sold her car in two days

unnecessarily. But I was clear about this final business.
And so I went to the "funeral home." My beloved
would not lie here. Not upstairs with the palms anyway.
No funeral, no casket, no "viewing."

Immediate cremation was what we agreed on long ago,
thank goodness, since five weeks from diagnosis to
death, partly in coma, afforded no time for such talk.
The man threw a glance to the ceiling in shocked disbelief.

"No ashes?" as if I had aimed a lethal blow at
the undertaking trade. Surely I would want to place "her"
in a sacred place, if not on the mantel. Urns available for
the purpose. Prices vary.

I wanted only her ring, which sealed our troth when we
were young, before we knew what we were getting into,
but now binds me to a world unseen. I need not know
the time or place of this business.

Now I will my mind to think of other things, like cloud
formations, and my lists. I will not be scattering you
by the sea you loved so much, or into the moist earth
where the roses grow by the kitchen door.

But now you are truly gone, and I sit here in
darkness, conjuring a new meaning of place,
where form and substance are insignificant,
and time shall be no more.

*Rev. Charles Brackbill, eighty, sat by his wife's bedside for two weeks while she
was in a coma. From her cancer diagnosis to her death, Gloria, his wife of
thirty-three years, lived only five weeks. "I wrote her memorial service at bed-
side, and shortly thereafter I began to set my feelings to verse," Brackbill says.
"Family members who watch their loved one die suffer differently from cancer
patients. The pathway from darkness to light has its own stages and agonies,
and we all stumble down this path in different ways."*

Brackbill's poems have been published in Writers' Journal *(with a first
prize awarded in August 1999),* Creative Transformation, Journal of
Pastoral Care, Mennonite Life, *and* Monday Morning.

*Still active as a Presbyterian minister, Brackbill spent most of his career as
a broadcasting executive for the Presbyterian Church. He received many pro-
gramming awards for his work and was named a "Pioneer in Religious
Broadcasting" by an international organization. An author and lecturer,
Brackbill is now somewhat retired, indulging his long interest in reading and
writing poetry. He lives in Mountainside, New Jersey.*

NEPHROSTOMY TUBE SURGERY AT AGE THIRTY-FOUR

by Karin B. Miller

These nurses seem more like maternal dime-store clerks
than well-trained medical staff,
adept in the ins and outs of cancer.
Round, warm, jolly, a bit unkempt.
They don't inspire confidence.
One drops the pill you're supposed to take.
The other tries to lighten the mood with a joke, at her expense.
They're showing me how I will have to change your dressing,
where the tube will come out of your back,
where the urine will flow through the tube,
down your leg and into a sack velcro-ed to your ankle.
I try to listen, but inside my head
I am screaming.
I want to shove them aside, grab the gurney
and race you down the hall,
yelling "We don't belong here!"

An hour later, the surgery over.
They hand me the tubes, the bags, the instructions.
Then we are in the hall,
returning to chemo.
You are on the gurney,
pushed by some white-coated employee.
I shuffle alongside.
For now,
this is our life.

GREEK

by Karin B. Miller

Orchiectomy, nephrostomy, etoposide,
platinol, bleomycin, neupogen.
The words make a home for themselves in my mouth,
unpack their bags, put their feet up, flick on the TV.
"We're here for the long haul," they say. "Get used to us."

I make liars of them!
In just months, I spit them out.
They're gone.
Now I have to look them up in a book.
I can't remember and
I thank God.

Karin B. Miller, thirty-six, started the Cancer Poetry Project in 1998 following her husband's diagnosis of and successful treatment for testicular cancer, which took the unusual form of a football-sized tumor in his abdomen. "Over the years I had gotten away from writing poetry on a regular basis, but when Thom's diagnosis coincided with my pregnancy, poetry provided the only outlet to say what I was feeling. 'Nephrostomy Tube Surgery at Age Thirty-Four' describes one of the worst days I experienced as a caregiver. I just felt so helpless."

While Miller has had a number of poems published, this full-time writer and editor generally splits her time between corporate contract work and magazine writing. "Leading this project has been a huge blessing in my life, a daily reminder of how fortunate my family is. For now, at least, we can speak of cancer in the past tense."

Miller lives with her husband and darling daughter in a 113-year-old house in St. Louis Park, Minnesota.

ODDS

by Jane Eaton Hamilton

You are thirty-four. You understand that your chances of
turning thirty-five are only adequate, but worth hoping on, and
that the chances of your turning forty are remote. The things
you appreciate are smaller than the things your friends
appreciate. The pulp of an apple. The dead petal of a tulip.
An ant crawling on a lit light bulb. Ugly men, stupid TV sitcoms.
You appreciate lottery tickets especially, but never buy them.
You laugh. You ignore the jolt of never again wearing a low-cut
gown, of never again being unsure how mammography is done.
Or why.

---

*"When I wrote this poem, I was thinking of friends and loved ones who
have suffered through breast cancer," says Jane Eaton Hamilton, forty-six.
"More recently, breast cancer touched my life when my long-term partner, Joy
Masuhara, developed it in 1998." Today, Joy goes dragonboating with a
group of Vancouver breast cancer survivors called Abreast in a Boat.
"Dragonboats are long boats seating about twenty-five paddlers. There are
breast cancer-related dragonboating teams around the world. Despite lymph
node removals, they train and compete to show the public that there is life
and ability after a breast cancer diagnosis."*

*An award-winning, full-time writer, Hamilton is the author of the
children's book* Jessica's Elevator *(Beach Holme, 1989); a book of short
stories,* July Nights *(Douglas and McIntyre, 1992); and two poetry books,*
Body Rain *(Brick Books, 1991), in which the poem "Odds" first appeared,
and* Steam-Cleaning Love *(Brick Books, 1993). Shorter works – in such
publications as* The New York Times, Maclean's, Seventeen, *and various
anthologies – have won numerous awards and have been cited by the*
Pushcart Prize *and* Best American Short Stories.

*Hamilton lives with her partner and their two children, Sarah and
Meghann, in Vancouver, British Columbia, where they dance and garden.*

The Cancer Poetry Project

A LESSON
In memory of Becky Bender,
February 12, 1952–April 18, 1995

by Judy Rohm

At a breast cancer rally she rises
above sixteen positive lymph nodes
to tell the world that cancer is a wakeup call
that resonates to the cell level.
It is a lesson taught to trembling hands
that squeeze from today a second cup of coffee
on a sunny deck with someone you love.
It is a slap that sends you flying from Michigan
to Cozumel because cancer teaches that snorkeling
coral reefs pays greater dividends than a savings account
and mowing summer grass can be postponed
for bike rides past wild flowers and country streams,
and vacuuming the carpet and washing the windows
are low priority items when a friend drops by to visit.
Cancer is not a gift but a lesson
full of seeing now and loving presently.

Judy Rohm, sixty-one, was inspired to write about her longtime partner and best friend, Becky Bender, after Bender addressed an American Cancer Society rally in Lansing, Michigan, in May 1993. Bender had been diagnosed with breast cancer the year before at the age of forty. She died in 1995. "Seeing how the experience of facing death transformed her, how she lived every day in her life, taught me a lot about courage," Rohm says.

Two years later, Rohm's "dear brother and only sibling" died of pancreatic cancer after a nine-month struggle. And in 1998, Rohm herself was diagnosed with advanced ovarian cancer. "What I have witnessed and experienced during the past eight years has been terrifying and transforming," says Rohm, who has written a collection of sixty-four cancer-themed poems.

Rohm is a retired educator with thirty-three years of experience teaching English, writing, and communication. She lives in Mason, Michigan.

CHOCOLATES

by Marjorie Woodbury

When he wakes with pain pounding
his spine, and it's still two hours
before she can give him the fat yellow capsule
he craves, she offers chocolates
instead. He runs his hand over cellophane,
and suddenly he, to whom nothing
has tasted good for weeks, rips
the box open, devours an orange cream,
then three more, before offering them
to her. Propped against the big bed's headboard,
knees drawn up, they eat chocolates
like children: testing centers for flavor, licking their fingers,
letting wrappers fall in the sheets.
He savors the sweet on his tongue,
and it lulls him, like her quiet talk
of gardening, the cats, groceries she must buy
the next day, until they sense
another night past. Turning from each other,
they breathe more easily, crumpled, fluted wrappers
rustling when they turn, the empty box between them.

Marjorie Woodbury died in 1993 at age fifty-three from leukemia. "Chocolates" is part of a seven-poem sequence called "Fast Ride," which she wrote about her uncle's death from lung cancer.

As a medical editorial advisor at the University of Virginia Medical Center, Woodbury encountered cancer patients at the hospital every day. She also lost her mother to cancer, as well as a friend and fellow employee at the hospital. "She had a deep capacity to empathize with the suffering of others, perhaps because of her own experience with loss," says Dana Roeser, her friend and literary executor.

Woodbury, who wrote all of her life (she published her first story at the age of twelve), completed her MFA degree at Warren Wilson College in Swannanoa, North Carolina. Prior to her death, her poems appeared in Poetry East, Zone 3, Iris, The Bennington Review, *and other publications. A number of her poems have been published posthumously.*

THE SEVEN SORROWS

by Nancy Madison Fitzgerald

1. KEEPING VIGIL IN THE ICU

After nine hours of surgery
you lay stapled, strapped,
red from blood,
yellow with iodine,
tubed, monitored, shuddering
amidst the others moaning, heaving,
wrestling with the angels down in Sheol.
Up until that time
you said you'd be fine
and I believed you.

Now your eyes,
which had always steadied mine,
looked out in terror.

I held your feet and read the Psalms.
"If I make my bed in Sheol, God is there."
"God's heart is the first to break."
"No coward Soul is mine."
The lies I learned to live by.

2. WAITING FOR REPORTS

The sounds of nurses,
some with wings,
some thumped and banged,
attentive, tuned, listening for the god,
the doctor, the savior,
the brisk clip of his footstep,
the bevy at his heels.
He did not look at me,

but fussed around the bed,
that high altar where you lay
in pain, waiting, waiting, for reports.

3. CRYING IN THE TUB

At home you sat soaking in the tub.
I brought a candle and sherry,
sought your eyes.
You held the glass to toast us.
The beauty of your body bruised,
the steam, the sherry, our love.

4. TOXINS IN THE BRAIN

When the toxins hit his brain
he went wild.
Restless, tormented,
wandered through the house
like a muddled bear, turned
the kitchen faucet on,
stood shuffling there.
I followed him deep,
deep into this cave,
calling to the one he was before.
But he was gone.

5. DAYS OF STUPOR

The radio played Bach
as he journeyed out
toward the other side
held captive by his body.
Hours and days of silence,
then his eyes sought mine.
"That's a Bach Cantata in
D Minor."

6. THE GENTLE FIREMEN ARRIVE

Downstairs once too often
for a meal
we could not get him up again.
The firemen came quickly,
picked him up right
in his chair and carried him to bed.
They tucked him tenderly.
"Thank you, gentlemen," he said.
They stood silent in the sadness.

7. HELPING TO OPEN THE DOOR

"Help me open the door. Help me.
Help me end this agony."
"I cannot."
More morphine, more morphine, more.
Some water from the cup
to your lips, to my lips.
Someone on the other side,
hear our plea, please
hear our plea.

MARCH 29, 1985

by Nancy Madison Fitzgerald

He died the same night as Chagall,
floated up away from her
as she tried to anchor him
with a final kiss.

Now in racing skies she sees
acrobats in slants of white,
lovers drifting in the trees,
scarlet angels, flying fish,
vases full of flower moons,
swimmers in a sea of blossoms,
levitating brides and grooms.

When she sleeps, the purple village
rests beneath white lily stars.
Crested roosters watch at dawn
as cubes of morning light arise.

Nancy Madison Fitzgerald, fifty-eight, wrote her first poem, "You Wore a Tie for Chemo," after her husband of twenty years died of bladder cancer. Jack had lived for twelve years after diagnosis, and had undergone a cystectomy (bladder removal). He died after the cancer spread to his liver. "Writing down those painful memories helped me to make sense of them, to contain their potency, their ability to sweep me into circles of grief over and over and over again."

Now a widely published poet, Fitzgerald teaches creative writing at The College of St. Scholastica in Duluth, Minnesota. Her new chapbook, Poems I Never Wrote, *will be published by Poetry Harbor in 2001.*

Fitzgerald lives with husband Jerry Agnew, whose wife Eleanor also died of cancer. Together they have raised six children and now spoil and pamper their large, shaggy dog.

SURVIVAL DIPTYCH

by David Graham

1. ONE YEAR ANNIVERSARY

Nothing graspable. Rather the sift of fine sand
over all: bedclothes, book jackets, mirrors.
A slight grit in food, haze on the steps.
I had thought my adversary would appear
outright, wrestle me like angel and fool,
but day after day I gaze dumbly
at our windy black walnut sweeping and plunging
yet going nowhere. Just suffering in place.

Turns out I can't wait and weep both,
can't make diagnosis any sort of solution.

2. CONTENTMENT

Not, as I had dreamed, the flush of wine
or heat of bed. No electric plunge
of sled down icy hill. Rather
the sleeping breath of a walked dog
curled now at my feet. Merely the sound
of my wife humming in the bathroom
her pre-work arias. A moment
unaccountably crystalline, winter edging
the panes, and even the fact of cancer
just a fact this blazing day.

David Graham, forty-eight, wrote these poems "as part of my own therapy in dealing with the effects this disease has brought into our lives." Graham's wife, Lee Shippey, was diagnosed with breast cancer, had a radical mastectomy on one breast in 1997, then had another mastectomy later that year, followed by chemotherapy. She now is doing well.

"In this poem, the fact of Lee's cancer weighs on my mind and colors my mood, no matter what, and thus threatens to leach a lot of the pleasure out of life," he says. "On the other hand, I gradually realize that it is still possible to find pleasure, often in the smallest things."

Graham's poetry has appeared in numerous journals and in five collections, most recently Stutter Monk *(Flume Press, 2000), which includes "Survival Diptych." A retrospective collection,* David Graham's Greatest Hits 1975–2000, *is forthcoming (Pudding House Publications, 2001).*

Graham and his wife live in Ripon, Wisconsin, where he teaches English.

ELEGY

by Tad Richards

No breasts,
you said,
No breasts. I want you to see
what I look like.

Then you turned,
hands down at your side,
the razed, scarred, lost battlefield
of your chest, toward me.

Can you look at it?
Does it disgust you?

You knew
how much I loved young girls
with their breasts like snowflakes,
loved them as much as
they bored you, with their self-absorption,
as much as you loved young men,
the beautiful, quick, self-assured ones –

No breasts, Tad!
Can you look at it?
Does it disgust you?

No way I could have hid it, if it had.
It was too late for that,
and there was so little left of you;
and no matter how gently I kissed your scars
the satyr cancer still ate you from inside.

The Cancer Poetry Project

Tad Richards, sixty-one, says this is the only poem he's ever written about cancer. "It's a poem from my youth. I had come east to stay with Noelle, maybe fifteen or twenty years older than me, to work on writing the English language dialogue to Costa-Gravas' movie State of Siege. *She had undertaken the project and was under extraordinary pressure to finish it before she died. So we were tied together by the intensity of work. The event described in this poem took place one afternoon. I guess she needed to know that she was still sexual. It was important to her not to hide her body, but to show it and have it embraced. She died within a week after delivering the finished product."*

Poems by Richards have appeared in Laurel Review, Carolina Quarterly, Chiron Review, Plastic Tower, *and others. His collection,* My Night with the Language Thieves *(Victoria, 2001), includes "Elegy."*

Richards lives in Saugerties, New York, on the grounds of the monumental environmental sculpture Opus 40. *He is married to Patricia and has three daughters, two stepchildren, and seven grandchildren.*

VALENTINE'S DAY, 1975

by Patricia A. Joslin

No white linen tablecloth. No white candles twinkled. No string quartet
played sweet music
as we dined.
Even the meal was nothing more than usual fare. But we were in love.

We were quiet through dinner, knowing that all we wanted to say had
been said
many times over. So we waited, staring into approaching night with nothing
more than the fluorescent track over your bed
to shed light on the situation.

You were pale and frail by then, your skin stretched thin over fragile
bones. Your hair hadn't grown back so you wore that ill-fitting wig
rather than show your baldness. The doctor arrived for
evening rounds. Dark circles under his eyes,
lab coat wrinkled under his arms.
A long day – as always.

He pulled the old straight-backed chair
from the corner of the room, so
close that his knee grazed
mine. I sat beside you
on the bed. The message
wasn't news, really.
He cried with us,
real tears.

Later that night Ann came to hug you.
She was your favorite, I recall.
She did her best to cheer you, even decorated your IV pole
with red paper hearts.
She pinned one to your chest and told you she loved you because
you had heart.
She cried too,

then took your blood pressure with the familiar black cuff that hung on the wall.

So long ago – yet the white room and red hearts fill a black space that suffocates me still.

Patricia A. Joslin, fifty, lost Keith, her high school sweetheart, to lymphoma when he was twenty-six and she was twenty-five. They had been married less than two years when he was diagnosed; he died two years later. "It was a life-time ago – and since that time I have been blessed with a wonderfully rich family life with my second husband," Joslin says. "But the memories, of course, remain a part of me.

"On Valentine's Day 1975, Keith was told to prepare for his death, which would be weeks away. I wrote the poem because I wanted to remember those emotional moments in vivid detail, and to somehow address their reality. With the writing of that poem, I felt a sense of peace." Joslin began writing poetry at The Loft in Minneapolis a few years ago; this is her first published poem.

A former school principal and teacher, Joslin currently works as the director of training for a software consulting firm. She lives with her husband of twenty-four years, Roy, in Minnetonka, Minnesota. Daughter Jennifer is an English major at Davidson College. Son Michael is a high school student.

RICHARD LEAVING

by Ann Sanfedele

There was never enough time to say goodbye
Although goodbye was part of every day, well,
More precisely, every night between larger and
Larger portions of the bitter brown liquid needed
To hold back the pain. Cracked and swollen lips
Reluctantly received the syringe at increasingly
Shorter intervals – but at least there were no needles,
No links to machines or hardware. His wish.

White tablets pulled me through it. Buzzers were
Scarcely needed, though, to wake me at precisely
Spaced hours; each waking filled with apprehension
That it would and wouldn't be the last time to abuse him
Briefly for his benefit. They told us there need never be
Pain and we believed them. We actually believed them.

The day before he left I bought $56 worth of
Chinese takeout. It wasn't planned. It just happened.
A mourning dove came into our living room to forage.
Truly. A spiny lizard appeared at the bedroom window
Resting long enough for Richard to get a final glimpse.
So everyone knew what the next day was. Even the nurses.

For days I had slept near him with a mirror angled so
That I could see his face and know. He could not speak
Above a whisper; his arms could not bear the weight
Of his hands to beckon and none of the rest of him could
Move at all. But at least he was in no pain and had his wits.
That's what they all said: there was no reason for pain.

His vitals told the nurses we need not force the Rodinol
On him further. Liquids outflowing in plastic tubes bore
Witness. He wanted me to sleep. I wanted to say goodbye.

He whispered we had said goodbye so many times. He
Managed to close his forefinger and thumb on my hand.

Somewhere between midnight and two I woke. His eyes
were closed. I didn't know where he was. I slept more.
At four I called the hospice. The splendid nurse arrived.
She helped me get him into his St. Louis Cardinals T-shirt.
I brushed back his hair and held him in my arms until they
Came with that undignified blue plastic bag to haul him off.
They were out the door before I remembered the button
His daughter had given him for Christmas the past year.
The one that said "If you're looking for me, I just left."

---

*Ann Sanfedele, sixty-four, wrote this poem two years after losing her lover of
thirteen years to prostate cancer. "This poem is a kind of clarification for me
and a way of putting the event behind me. But it also has elements of a
warning to those who may need to come to terms with the reality of witness-
ing someone suffer from this slow and painful passing."*

*Sanfedele has had her poetry and photographs included in a number
of publications. Retired from computer programming, she is concentrating
on her photography and honing her web-site designing skills. She lives in
New York City.*

MOURNING DOVES

by Rebecca Wee

They thrive in the walls of the attic,
nesting, love-moans, arguments.
At first I liked it, their lives
next to mine yet concealed.
Today I want them gone.

They live and you are dead.

They sleep, strut, have babies
under the eaves, out of the rain,
while you are grey ash and bone
bits in a green blown-glass
bottle downstairs.

If I weren't so full of the chasm
you left, I would take an ax
to the walls, I would
slaughter them.
And it wouldn't change a thing.

WIDOW

by Rebecca Wee

Scorched word, I will not have it. Nor
will I say to myself in the monstrous bed
that you are gone.

Austere. Taut and fallow,
such threadbare self-containment.
What is left.

The brokenness confounds
those who come with kind hands.
The pieces so many, one cannot

be what one was.
After howling and coagulation,
after ashes

and dreams of knives, gas stoves,
the pill bottles, the one step into traffic,
after this

there are the next mornings
with their new old gall,
and the widow lives

on oblivion no matter how
many neighbors bring bread
and soup. No matter

how flawless the jonquils or cards
or friends who arrive with their arms out.
No matter how fair the day.

You went from the bed without me, love,
yellow rot in the sheets, the glare
and drone of machines gone still –

you left me. Gutted. Charred.
Our separate and miserable griefs,
your dying and my living

death – the sallow hallways,
my slow-motion race
to reach you, elevators oblivious,

the horror careening against months
of horror until it became something
quite new. I believed you would live.

I believed I would not be a widow
at thirty-six, my lips useless
without yours.

I hate how I can't bear it.
How each day I find
again I can't bear it.

My lamentations futile
in the world. Tedious pain,
the embarrassment of grief

that goes on. I want to tell
the woman in line for cigarettes
of your staggering beauty,

your tenderness and dry wit.
I want to explain
I wasn't always like this –

I belonged, I fit, I would
have looked you in the eye.
I want the dentist to know

what it was to love you,
how new I became in your arms.
How brilliant you remain

in my story of our hours.
You were that luminous brief gift,
my rapture and vows and home

at last. Yes, the widow screams
and screams through the nights.
What is left cannot be touched.

---

*Rebecca Wee, thirty-eight, has recently returned to writing and teaching since
the death of her husband, Michael Hudson, in 1998 after a nineteen-month
battle with leukemia; he was thirty-seven years old. "Michael believed fiercely
in my poetry, and I find now that it's one way for me to face his death and
my grief," she says. "It's one way of trying to endure, I suppose, even if I can't
make 'sense' of what happened to us.*

*"I believe poetry rewards and sustains us precisely because it doesn't look
away from our deepest, hardest, most central emotions. We live in a culture of
avoidance. We want quick fixes, sound bites. Our attention spans are limited.
Good poems don't accommodate that – they demand full engagement with the
monstrous and exquisite range of human experiences."*

Wee's poems have been published in The Iowa Review, Ploughshares,
The Plum Review, The Sonora Review, *and other literary journals. Wee has
received eight poetry awards, including a fellowship from the Minnesota State
Arts Board and the 2000 Hayden Carruth Award for New and Emerging
Poets. Her first collection of poems,* Uncertain Grace, *is forthcoming from
Copper Canyon Press.*

*Wee lives in Rock Island, Illinois, where she teaches creative writing, lit-
erature, and composition at Augustana College.*

THE CANCEROUS CELL

by James Doyle

The cancerous cell
turns a page and then another page.
It can't put the book down. It reads
faster and faster. It will read
through the night until the story
is finished. The doctor says
don't worry, we have ways to cure
its obsession, stop it from going on, turn
it towards a different ending, its own.
The book of your body won't be
read in a single night, in a few
months, in a year. It will go on and on
like an epic, until it has exhausted
itself, and all the possibilities, with its
knowledge, until it has taken in
enough worlds to become a universe.

Like creation itself the first cancer cell must
have come out of nothing, maybe when
the earth's crust was still bubbling over
with lava, before it got the idea of cooling;
maybe that far back; maybe later,
when single things were straining
to divide, to duplicate themselves,
and a runaway seed seemed a miracle,
a richness suddenly showered down on them;
or maybe that first cell was in the air
like a spore, waiting on the coastline
with its own, new definition of complexity
for the first life to crawl
out of the ocean. Maybe it was preserved
through the ice ages, pressed
at the center of mountains, so many

cocoons of sheer rock spun around it
while it waited for the sun, meaning
only good, to grow larger and closer
to the earth's surface again. Maybe one cell
after another rode time down all

its seasons, all its geological eras,
like leaves or pollen on a mountain
stream, now frozen in place, now
racing downhill to join the spring, mesh
with the thronging harvests of the fall.

It has taken all the time
in the world until now for us
to become literate. But it has paid
off. We can string together a line
of causes and effects from the first
parting of chaos to the final
judgment and call it science. We
can go far beyond Adam and Eve,
who only had to name the things
of Eden, and we can come up with words
like *cancer* which seem primeval
and newly-minted at the same time.
We can invent the intimacy of a biopsy
and pinpoint the precise moment
when the microscopic world of cells
opened like a gorge and we swayed
on its edge, growing dizzy, staring down
and down. In this case, 2:16 PM,
Tuesday, February 23, 1999.

In this poem, James Doyle, sixty-four, cites the exact moment when he and his wife of twenty-seven years, Sharon, were notified that she had uterine cancer. "I suspect all cancer patients and their loved ones have that first moment of notification stamped so vividly on their memories that there is no possibility of ever forgetting," he says. While much of "The cancerous cell" focuses on cancer's impersonal past, "there is no escaping the specific, personal notification. The poem ends with the necessity of facing this moment." Sharon underwent surgery, nine months of chemotherapy, and radiation treatment. Two years later, there is no sign of recurrence.

Doyle's work has appeared in more than two hundred journals, including The Berkeley Poetry Review, Chiron Review, The Cream City Review, Poetry, *and* The Ohio Review, *which first published "The cancerous cell." His most recent book is called* The Silk at Her Throat *(Cedar Hill Publications, 1999).*

Doyle spent twenty-six years teaching on the English faculty of the University of Northern Colorado, Greeley. He lives with wife Sharon in Fort Collins. They have five children and seven grandchildren. Sharon Doyle's poem, "There's not a book on how to do this" is found on page 52.

POEMS BY FAMILY MEMBERS

SONG

by Kevin Smith

tell me
if a woman enters
her local small-town
hospital
with two eyes, two ears,
two legs, two arms,
two breasts, one proud body
if the surgeons, the nurses,
the surgical technician,
the anesthesiologist
remove one small breast
then when she caresses
her naked body
will she hear all or half
the sparrow's sad sad song?

no
she will open
her mouth and
sing a song
of life.

"Watching my mother deal with her breast cancer diagnosis and mastectomy was truly a lesson in bravery," says Kevin Smith, thirty-six. "She wanted to do whatever she needed to do to continue with her life." Today, his mother enjoys a healthy life, and tests reveal her to be cancer free. Smith's poetry has been published in various journals, including Baybury Review *and* California Quarterly. *He lives in Cleveland, Oklahoma, where he works as a psychological clinician at a medium-security prison.*

SHE'S ALL RIGHT

by Darci D. Schummer

My brown-eyed girl is going to be okay.
She's going to dance until her feet blister –
floating, flying, gliding –
feeling her way across the stage like an olive-skinned angel.
My silly, singing, molasses-haired girl
is going to raise her strong voice in a cry of victory.
We're going to feel the summer sun on our backs again.
No disease, no sickness is gonna hurt
my childhood playmate,
my blood and my half,
my sister.

Darci D. Schummer, twenty, wrote "She's All Right" in honor of older sister Amy when she was diagnosed with Hodgkin's disease. "I knew she could make it through – knew that she could win," Schummer says. "She is one of the strongest, most beautiful people I have ever met. I wanted to write a poem to illustrate that." Amy is now cancer free and in excellent health.

Schummer, the youngest of eight children, is a creative writing major at the University of Wisconsin, Eau Claire. She has had a short story published in her university's literary magazine, NOTA.

CIGARETTES

by Suzanne Frischkorn

Beyond the doubt of shadows lingering,
the pine trees stretched into authorities
of mountains, molehills, mollusks
under the veil of a starry night
ten-year-olds in white, T-shirts, blue, jeans
grip Lucky Strikes
between dirt-streaked fingers
cheeks: soft, ripe
eyes: shiny, mean
smoke weaves a tapestry with pine needles
Beyond the doubt of shadows winding
into complexities
of deliverance, destruction, decay
fifty-year-old men in thin, cotton, gowns
grip Lucky Strikes
between yellow-stained fingers
cheeks: rough, sallow
eyes: dull, mean
smoke circles the intravenous
and dissipates in fluorescent lights

Suzanne Frischkorn, thirty-one, lost her brother to leukemia after a five-year struggle. "'Cigarettes' illustrates the cycle of addiction," Frischkorn says. "When visiting my brother in the hospital, I often saw men like those in my poem who continued to smoke despite having cancer." Her poem first appeared in the Journal of the American Medical Association (JAMA).

Frischkorn's poetry appears in such publications as The Isle Review, Orange Willow Review, *and* In Our Own Words – A Generation Speaks for Itself *(Vol. 2). She is also the author of two chapbooks,* Exhale *(Scandinavian Obliterati Press, 2000) and* The Tactile Sense *(Alpha Beat Press, 1996). She is the poetry editor of the online literary journal,* Samsara Quarterly.

Frischkorn lives with her husband and son in Stamford, Connecticut.

POEM OF THE WEEK

by Veneta Masson

A friend's sage advice:
>   *Just do what you can do*
>   *on a given day.*
So on days I can't pray
or pick up the phone
I send a poem.
>   Poem of the Weak,
>   I once accidentally called it.

I've sent Carver, Frost,
Sarton, Levertov,
Pastan, Olds and others –
my emissaries,
my cloud of witnesses.

Let these poets earn their keep.
Let them speak for me.
Let them enter the house
haunted by illness.
Let them open the doors
shut against fear.

For in trouble
the poem is strong medicine
like the wind that blows
where it wills,
like the serpent of brass
set upon a pole
in the wilderness.

During the years that her younger sister, Rebecca, was struggling with breast cancer, Veneta Masson, now fifty-seven, found refuge and sustenance in poetry. "As I began sending poems, my own and others', to Rebecca, I was amazed to discover how they opened a way to a deeper, stronger relationship."

Masson's poetry has appeared in The Sun, Lancet, *and* Nursing and Health Care Perspectives, *as well as several anthologies.* Rehab at the Florida Avenue Grill *(Sage Femme Press, 1999) is a chronicle in poems of Masson's thirty-five years as a nurse. She lives in Washington, D.C.*

NOT LISTENING

by Virginia Chase Sutton

The oncologist tells him *no more golf, it's*
112 degrees for chrissakes. It's 5 a.m. after
sprinklers have coated what's left of the grass
in a fury of haze and droplets. Pure passion.
Not chemo, not radiation, not his wife
calling *Bob, Bob, it's time to come in.* All
that matters is here: one little ball whizzing,
not connecting, shallow holes and bravely
numbered flags. He's wearing twenty-year-old
glasses, a new eccentricity, so I call him
Disco Dad. He likes it: memories of dusky leisure
suits, small snags on a floral polyester shirt,
wide collar brimming. Where was the tumor?
A pack of Kents stashed in his pocket, a cigarette
poking through tanned fingers. Early morning's
his time now, summer days dull and stupid,
blistering skin, a cap snug above his high forehead.
He aims past dry duck ponds, heat blazing
through the soles of his shoes. Whatever
he remembers is all uninterrupted surface,
like the silver thermometer today.

*"My dad loved golf; he played right up until his last hospitalization —
eighteen holes nearly every day," says Virginia Chase Sutton, forty-six.
"After having a heart transplant ten years ago, he was sure he could beat
lung cancer, too, right up until his last three days." Her father died at age
seventy-five in spring 2000.*

*Sutton, an award-winning poet, teaches English at Phoenix College. Her
manuscript, "Netting the Gaudy Pearls," has been a finalist in a number of
national poetry book competitions, including the National Poetry Series, the
Walt Whitman Award, the New Issues Poetry Prize, and the Marianne
Moore Poetry Prize. Last summer she was named a Bread Loaf Writers
Poetry Scholar. Her poetry has been published in such journals as* The Paris
Review, Ploughshares, *and* Antioch Review.

*Sutton is married, lives in Tempe, Arizona, and has two daughters in
high school.*

I WILL BREATHE AND BREATHE

by Jeanne Bryner

While the doctor says *bone tumors*
I will watch his nurse take you away for more x-rays.
You are five years old. Your father is golfing.
I will blink and remember a one-legged woman
skiing on TV.
I will change the words *chance of malignancy* to
mild blue skies.
The hump on your scapula is cauliflower.
The lump on your left leg, a frond.
You are a bowl of petals, and this, an awful wind.
I will burn the doctor's tumor book, run
from this office not knowing our destination.
I will tell your father a story about a wolf and a lamb,
a gate we did not close.
In the waiting room, children bald from chemo.
Your father's face hidden behind a magazine.
Your dolly's yarn hair, body of cloth – any flame
can take us. I will promise the tumor doctor
to harvest his thistle fields barehanded.
I will quit swearing. I will donate a kidney.
I will babysit the neighbors' retarded sons
while they visit Europe, Australia, Mars.
The doctor lifts you to his exam table, touches skin
where bone cells rage, drunken thugs in a cave.
When he says your name, it feels like calico,
soft and ready to cut.

Jeanne Bryner, forty-nine, wrote this poem after thirteen years of processing her daughter's diagnosis of multiple hereditary exostosis at age five. "It has a 5 to 25 percent chance of malignancy. So far, so good." she says. "In 2000, my daughter developed numbness and tingling in her left foot, and she began the whole gamut of tests again. This brought back my terror, and the poem was born."

Today, despite numbness and tingling, periodic tests, and tumors in the hips, legs, arms, fingers, spine, and left scapula, her daughter is doing fine. "To look at her, you'd never know."

An emergency room nurse, Bryner has had her prose and poetry published in West Branch, The Journal of Emergency Nursing, *and* Boomer Girls: Poems by Women from the Baby Boom Generation *(University of Iowa Press, 1999). She has two books,* Breathless *(Kent State University Press, 1995) and* Blind Horse *(Bottom Dog Press, 1999). In 1997, she received an Individual Artist Fellowship from the Ohio Arts Council. Bryner also teaches writing workshops for breast cancer survivors. "Working with them is a privilege and blessing in my life," she says.*

Bryner lives near a dairy farm in Newton Falls, Ohio, with her husband of thirty years, David, and their two children.

HISTORY

by Vera Kroms

When a cell beneath this skull
began to multiply, devouring his life
backwards, English, his last mental feast,
started disappearing from his speech, word
by word, like coins dropping through a hole
in his tongue. At night, he woke to Berlin
toppling in the distance. Three women
who called him father kept visiting.
The slide rule, which had calibrated
his ascent from farm boy to professor
became, for him, an artifact
from a forgotten race. In the end,
he was spooned the softest food, his mouth
receiving what he understood.

Vera Kroms, fifty-two, wrote "History" about her father as he was dying from brain cancer. "The process whereby he 'disappeared' as the cancer devoured his mind was both fascinating and profoundly distressing," she says. "This person whom I'd known all my life, whose European life comprised the stories I grew up on, retreated and retreated to a place where all of it – World War II and the Russian takeover of his home in Latvia – had never taken place. When a parent regresses in memory to a time before you are born, it is a startling, lonely place to be. Poetry allowed me to address this and to celebrate the complexity of this man's life at the same time."

Kroms' poetry has appeared in Web Del Sol, Southern Poetry Review *and* Worcester Review. *She has studied with several poets in the Boston-Cambridge area, most recently with Lucie Brock-Broido. Kroms lives in Brighton, Massachusetts, and works as a computer programmer.*

The Cancer Poetry Project

MOTHER, I AM FEELING MYSELF SLIP

by Luissa Joy Chekowsky

mother, I am feeling myself slip

into the times you have died before
and I am afraid

of genetics
biology

like you
i am afraid
of the splitting of atoms
osmosis
mutations
doctors
of the word
cells

since i first heard
i have been dreaming in colored diagrams
and i still don't know how one could have turned
into two and four and
more

i am swallowing hard
like you have been doing for years
but you with your eyes open
welcoming

and i am still closed
dwelling on where the first one
came from

was it from
god

did he place violently the first cancer
that i am watching eat you a piece at a time
with the only cure to cut or to burn

or maybe you were blessed to die slowly
into heaven
each offering accepted by the angels
gradually being pieced together again
waiting there for you

because you have learned how to die right
because from the very beginning

you were chosen
to
simply

disappear

Luissa Joy Chekowsky, now twenty-seven, was nine years old when her mother was first diagnosed with breast cancer. On her tenth birthday, her mother had her first mastectomy. When the cancer returned nine years later, and Chekowsky herself was diagnosed with a precancerous condition, she wrote this poem. "It was pretty frightening, and more intense because I was going through it with my mom," she says. "It made me feel even more sympathetic toward my mother. Her cancer was incredibly aggressive and spread quickly from lymph nodes to bone, to lung, and to brain." Her mother died at age sixty-three, when Chekowsky was twenty-two.

Two years prior, Chekowsky's parents heard her read this poem at a coffee-house near the University of Central Florida, where she was studying creative writing. "It was one of the most powerful moments of my life," she says. "I am still grateful that we talked about her death – how much she would be missed by me and how much she would miss me, too. I know that my writing about her facilitated these conversations, and I'm so glad for that."

A former reporter for Details *magazine, Chekowsky now works in marketing and publicity for* Time Out New York *in New York City.*

BIG SALE TODAY

by Carol Kapaun Ratchenski

No one times the disposable
Diapers right or the formula
Or baby wipes. Always
Half packages remain.

Every mother's lap empties out.
Still, mine did so in a second,
In the space that should have
Divided one breath from the next.

Becoming silence forever.
Today, beside two car seats, one crib,
Three boxes of board books,
One stroller, one swing set,

Pooh Bear, Tigger and Owl.
Unopened play dough jars,
Three-bedroom house and van,
All the unsung nursery rhymes,

And dreams of Little League wins,
I long to put my body –
Arms, hips and singing lungs –
on my garage sale today.

In the yard and for sale now, cheap.
But no one wants to buy from us.
Might be selling dark luck.
I change the sign by noon.

Dead child's toys for free, help yourself.
I go into my vacant house
Then back out, add in bold
Cancer is not catching.

Carol Kapaun Ratchenski, forty-one, is a poet whose son Kevin was diagnosed with cancer the day after his second birthday. Eight months later, he lost his battle with cancer. "My entire life, including my writing," she says, "has been blessed by the experience of knowing Kevin and witnessing his endless joy and courage, even in leaving this world behind."

Ratchenski's poetry has appeared in Gypsy Cab, Willow Street, North Dakota Quarterly *and* Red Weather. *She lives on the prairie of North Dakota with husband David and son Adam.*

READY OR NOT

by David Sten Herrstrom

I am merely an apprentice.
My daughter's the master of pain,
her mother the usual partner
in this Infusion Room business.
But today I hold her hand,
or she holds mine.
A man in an easy chair
with a sack above his head
as if it were a lamp
and this his living room
chatters on. Shining liquid
drips into his veins.
"It's pictures," he says, "pictures
that crowd out cancer."
And he deliberately remembers
summer hide-and-seek
in sharp dune grass, hanging
the same picture each week
which no one has seen.
A nurse swabs to the shadow
of tan above my daughter's breast
where a port to her heart
mounds the skin. We find
my one hand grasping hers
firmer than comfort requires
for either of us. The other
sweats in my pocket
clasping a pack of Life Savers,
ready for when she asks.
The nurse arms a needle with poison
then thrusts through the port pumping
to waste cells that terrorize
the outposts of my daughter's body.

The Cancer Poetry Project

The plunger keeps on firing.
Cells are flushed from the hills
driven to the sea and killed,
while the nurse counts,
my daughter
making movies in her mind –
alley alley oxen free –
my hand still in my pocket
clinging to the Life Savers.

David Sten Herrstrom, fifty-four, says he wrote this poem out of anger, love, and fear. "Anger that my daughter had to suffer such relentless pain, love for my daughter that compelled me to share a part of her pain, and fear that the gap between the pain I felt and the pain she felt was unbridgeable – meaning I could not love enough. So in the end, I had to make a praise song to my daughter's courage to preserve this brave moment otherwise gone." The good news is that his daughter is doing well and it has been ten years since her last chemo treatment.

Poems by Herrstrom have appeared in Nimrod *and* US1 Worksheets, *among other literary journals. His book,* Jonah's Disappearance *(Ambrosia Press), with drawings by Jacob Landau, was published in 1990.*

Herrstrom works for Citigroup in Manhattan. He lives with his wife in Roosevelt, New Jersey, where he serves as president of the Roosevelt Arts Project.

AFTER THE DIAGNOSIS

by Carolyn Hall

There are fewer birds, he says, now that the tree is gone
the fifty-year-old Chinese elm that shaded the deck
cut down – of necessity, but against his will –
he would have it still standing.

Paler, perhaps, and thinner
his shoulders planed to a narrower beam
he's little changed from the last time I saw him –
before the doctor said, *get your affairs in order.*
("They've been in order twenty years," he said, just *like* him.)
It's been months since he's really felt well
a "bug" he thought, picked up in Mexico
bragging about weight loss
as if it were his intention.
Still, until the words were spoken
he went to the office each day as he has for sixty years.
It is the *words* that have made the trip from home to work
too much; house to mailbox
too much; indoors to out
too much.

Feet up on the ottoman
hands clasped across his belly
chins folded into his collar,
his eyes disappear behind heavy lids
perhaps watching cells multiply
somewhere beneath his white leather belt.

How can he be dying? He isn't even lying down.

Carolyn Hall, sixty, wrote this poem for her father-in-law after he was diagnosed with liver cancer. He died only a few weeks later. "It has always seemed a great mystery to me: One minute we are alive, the next minute we are not," she says. "More than anything, this poem is about my struggle to come to terms with that existential mystery."

Hall lives in San Francisco with her husband of thirty-one years. Their twenty-year-old daughter is a college student on the East Coast. Hall gave up her career as a graphic designer six years ago and has since focused on writing creative nonfiction, fiction, and poetry.

LUCKY

by Tony Gloeggler

I show up on Sunday,
throw a load of laundry
into the washer. My mother
keeps busy in the kitchen.
I sit on the couch, read
newspapers until some game
comes on TV. My brother's
upstairs, still sleeping
last night off. The smell
of sauce simmers, fills
the house. My sister
and her kids are already

a half hour late. Mom
plops down next to me.
She's sucking on lemon drops,
trying to stop smoking
again. We won't mention
her recent hospital stay,
the endless tests, the guarded
prognosis, how the room
grew quiet and our faces
turned red when I helped
with her bedpan and sponge-
bathed her the first time.
I slip off my sneakers,
stretch out my legs and lay
my head in her lap.

Wednesday, she had another
test. This time, no traces
of cancer were found. I close
my eyes, feel her fingers

twirl my thinning hair.
She says she's getting up
early tomorrow morning, filling
her pocket book with rolls
of quarters, buying a ticket
on the Atlantic City Special
and riding this lucky streak
until her right arm falls off.

Tony Gloeggler, forty-six, says he used everyday details to say something about his relationship with his mother in "Lucky," which first appeared in The Ledge. *"My mom is alive, well, and still happily losing money to the Atlantic City slots," he reports.*

Gloeggler's work has appeared in journals and anthologies. His first chapbook, One on One, *won the Pearl Poetry Prize in 1998 and was published by Pearl Editions the following year. His full-length manuscript,* One Wish Left, *is forthcoming from Pavement Saw Press in 2001.*

Gloeggler runs a group home for developmentally disabled men in Brooklyn, New York.

PALM SUNDAY

by Charles Oberkehr

You rode triumphant
on a borrowed ass,
as only you could.
Dilettante
of the understated,
obscurity
the theme of
your best work.

My nephew comes forward today
self-consciously.
Bald from chemotherapy,
wearing a hat
to the altar,
to be confirmed.
And every other boy
wears one too.

It's true,
each moment must arrive
at its own hosanna,
welling up from the eloquence
of stones;
kneeling together
in the glass-stained light
as they greeted you once,
taking what was close at hand,
throwing it into the road
in front of you.

Charles Oberkehr, forty-four, was moved by a sense of helplessness to write this poem. "I was unable to attend my nephew's confirmation, but I heard about the gesture made by these boys. Like them, I was looking for a way to connect with him and perhaps help defeat the isolating effects of cancer." Oberkehr's nephew and godchild is in remission after a long stint of chemotherapy.

Oberkehr is an ordained pastor of the Evangelical Lutheran Church in America, serving a congregation in York, Pennsylvania. On the side, he is an award-winning writer, with poetry and essays published in the Palo Alto Review, Beauty for Ashes Poetry Review, California Quarterly, *and* Eclectic Rainbows. *He also writes an occasional column for the* York Sunday News.

Oberkehr is married, with two teenage sons and three stepdaughters.

FIVE-YEAR ANNIVERSARY
For my mother

by Kymberly Stark Williams

He remembers the day with roses,
one for each healthy year, five pink buds,
not red. Red reminds too much
of blood, the counting of cells,
veins that tired of needles and retreated.
But she is here, to take in his arms tonight
And tell her she is still beautiful.
He could say *more beautiful,* but then
he would have to explain what he cannot:
the shorn hair which seems a halo,
the light which emanates
from between the seams of her puckered scar,
or how her missing breast has not made her
half a woman, but rather, half an angel.
And lucky for him, the most practical
of angels: one who endures,
simply for the price of human love.

*Kymberly Stark Williams, twenty-eight, began to see her mother in a differ-
ent light after her mother's diagnosis of breast cancer. "I saw her as mortal,
of course, but also as a woman with amazing inner strength," Williams says.
"I was touched by my father's gentleness and support, and how he went so far
as to celebrate the anniversary of her surgery." Her mother has now celebrat-
ed her twelfth cancer-free anniversary.*

*Williams is a graduate of Sarah Lawrence College, where she studied
writing and edited* The Sarah Lawrence Review. *She works for Barnes and
Noble and lives with her partner, Erin, in Cherry Hill, New Jersey.*

A MOTHER'S DESPAIR

by Mary H. Amundsen

The day the doctor cut open my daughter
and told us, "Cancer"
I washed windows.
Every window in her house.
Ferociously and with anger
I sobbed my grief
onto every flyspeck, fingerprint
and unwanted spot
My fingers working beside the surgeon's
and when we were done
the windows and her body were clean.
She had no fertility left.
The windows were spotless.

Mary H. Amundsen, sixty-three, is a breast cancer survivor. Her husband has survived sinus cancer, her daughter has overcome ovarian cancer, and her daughter-in-law is currently being treated for bladder cancer. All of these experiences have pushed her to write a good deal of cancer-related poetry.

"Since childhood, I have written poetry to process my feelings and see things in a different way," she says. "Poetry is a comfort and companion that I can access at any time to express what is in my heart."

Amundsen, a retired nurse and counselor, volunteers her time to work with groups of cancer patients. She lives with her husband in Rochester, Minnesota.

SHAPE SHIFTER

by Scott Wiggerman

You waste no time. I'll give you that.
While grandmother's hull folds in on itself,
shrivels with tumors and chemicals,
I await the call to fly off to her funeral.

But you couldn't wait for another victim.
You crawled in bed with my youngest brother,
unfurled yourself while he lay dreaming,
and spread your shadow over his esophagus.
They say the way to a man is through his stomach,
but you've perfected every technique;
no organ is exempt from your dark embrace.

When your fingers clasped my mother's throat,
her voice immediately dropped several registers.
Teams of doctors loosened your grasp.
She didn't end up with an artificial voice box,
but I hear your echo when she speaks.

I was the next to escape your clutches,
and you left me off rather painlessly,
a bite on the leg, black as a horsefly.
Not that I haven't taken your visit seriously.
I check my skin with the diligence of a curator;
like you, I'm forced to stay in the shade.

With my father, you attacked the prostate,
spread your scaly fingers up his dark cavity
and pushed down like a rusty piston.
A buckshot of radioactive pellets chased you off;
yet you lurk in the air like a scavenger.
Circling my family in a restless gyration,
you'll be gorging again too soon.

Scott Wiggerman, forty-six, is no stranger to the threat of cancer. "It does seem to 'circle my family in a restless gyration,'" he says. "Somehow, most of us have survived, but we're still aware of cancer and how quickly it could turn on us again. Our lives are infused with cancer memories."

Wiggerman, a poet and a librarian with the Austin Independent School District, lives in Austin, Texas, with his partner, David Meischen. His first full-length book is Vegetables and Other Relationships *(Plain View Press, 2000), which includes "Shape Shifter."*

A FANTASY (THIRTY YEARS LATER)

by Mary Gorder

I have a fantasy
each time I drive up 7th Street
and see neat houses
with tulips growing in front yards and lilacs blooming

and the park on 7th Street
where children play and
you can sit if you want
and watch baseball teams rally to win.

In my fantasy
I buy a house on 7th Street in 1969,
the white one with the double garage,
a fenced-in yard,
and a dormer with lace curtains, tucked under the eaves.

Sis comes to stay with me
in my home on 7th Street.
She sits on the front step in an easy chair
and listens to music, soothing.
We read books about positive thinking and
eat cancer-fighting tomatoes and apricots.
The sun sends healing rays and
neighbors come by to say
Hi, how are you? and
energy flows to my sister sitting
there on the stoop on 7th Street.

Sis gets well in the white house
with the tulips growing and lilacs blooming.
We walk in the park across the street
and watch baseball teams rally to win.

She returns to children and the prairie farm
where she belongs,
so life for us can be sane and painless
In my fantasy.

Mary Gorder, fifty-seven, lost her older sister to ovarian cancer in 1969. After a three-year battle, she left behind a family of six children. "It was a horrendous experience, one that none of us who shared it will forget. I have found that writing, both journaling and poetry, still helps ease the pain and loneliness after thirty years." This is her first published poem.

Gorder, a retired elementary educator, lives in Coon Rapids, Minnesota.

SELF-EXAMINATION

by Clinton B. Campbell

Cowardly and with trepidation
I read the latest news.
Ballplayer, Cancer, Testicular.
"Examine yourselves," doctors advise.
I cross my legs right over left
trying to hide my fear.

My mate does not respond
as sweat runs down my face.
And late at night when
she's asleep I run my hands
inside my shorts and hold
on tight a real long time.
I'm glad these hands have never
done hard work as ten smooth
fingers fondle this old scrotum,
benign and hanging loose.

Turkey-skins, goose-pimpled
like sandpaper number 39.

I wonder, do my daughters
check their breasts
the way their mother does
the first of every month?
With one arm raised
she checks for change,
her face becomes a worry
hoping not to find
what she is looking for.

Now I feel for swellings
and if I find a pea-
sized lump, will they

compress my private parts,
do a scrotogram and push
and shove and yank until
they crack like walnuts?
Again I cross my legs,
this time left over right.

Clinton B. Campbell, sixty-five, is like many people who take new precautions or call for a doctor appointment after a loved one is diagnosed with cancer. It was the cancer diagnosis of an athlete that moved him to write this particular poem, which was first published in the journal Exit 13.

"Poetry is the original language of the human race," says Campbell, who took his first writing class at age fifty. A former restaurateur, Campbell now devotes his time to writing.

Campbell's work has appeared in several periodicals and anthologies, including Writer's Digest, Journal of New Jersey Poets, *and* Without Halos. *Campbell is married to fine-art photographer Karen M. Peluso. The couple lives in Ocean City, New Jersey, where Campbell is a fourth-generation resident.*

IN THE MIRROR

by John Grey

I watch you watching you.
I'm praying you see yourself beautiful,
not thin and drawn.
I'm wanting you to say to yourself,
"Ah, what eyes!"
as if they're about
to leap upon the next moment
of your life
like jockeys on the back of stallions.
I don't want the still bright green
to be dull gray stones
that slowly sink
to the bottom of your sockets.
You linger there
and that's hopeful.
With enough willpower,
you can make a lifetime
out of lingering.

John Grey, forty-five, wrote this poem in response to the death of his sister from bone cancer.

An Australian-born poet, playwright, and musician, Grey has had recent work published in Passages North, Hawaii Pacific Review, *and* South Carolina Review.

Grey lives in Providence, Rhode Island, where he works in data processing.

MOTHER EULOGY

by Shannon Sexton

I.

It began
as a small seed,
a small lump
under the armpit.

The doctor said, nothing wrong. Healthy
as an apple.
Thirty-nine
is too young
anyway.

II.

Trading Merry Christmas for *fuck you*
for the first time in her life,
she said *fuck you* to the pain
rippling through her
like an explosion.
To her husband,
working late hours,
avoiding
visits and sons –
and cracking jokes.
To the
gynecologist
who told her
the lump in her breast
was not malignant.

To the mammogram
that reinforced
his deadly diagnosis.

III.

Nine months later,
her struggle spread out
like bedsheets –
bald head, swollen
breast, arm. Fat
fingers clasping the other hand
are twice its size.

In her final weeks, a woman
throwing fists
in the eye of a storm.

IV.

The doctors said two years
but they lied. They lied.

It takes so much
to kill a mother.

"Not yet forty, Aunt Chrissie found the lump in her breast a year before the diagnosis, but her doctor waved her off, calling the lump another cyst; her mammogram did not detect the cancer. It was every woman's nightmare," says Shannon Sexton, twenty-three. "But she never lost her commitment to motherhood, and she gave thanks for a painless trip to the bathroom, the sight of her children's faces by her hospital bed, the touch of their hands to hers.

"Aunt Chrissie died with honor, I cannot tell you how. She will always be a role model for me, a selfless soul who I dearly hope is laughing somewhere at the memory of a shopping center in a small Ohio town blessed with Christmas snow, and two grown sisters giggling, bobbing heads, and bouncing up and down the aisles, so happy to be alive."

"Mother Eulogy" was first published in Inside Grief *(Wise Press, 2001).*

A recent graduate from Hiram College in Hiram, Ohio, Sexton works at the Case Western Reserve University Law School Library, writing and reading in her spare time. She lives in Cleveland, Ohio.

ADAGIO FOR GINNY

by Karen Leahy

When I see my brave, bald sister
stumble over stones of fear
on this hard path she did not choose,
I search my own heart for courage
and try to hold her steady
with words I hope carry hope.
I'd like to be for a day
the magical mother
who could kiss her on the brow
and make her brain all better.
She wants more years
to live out dreams
she's just getting around to.

Oh Great Beating Heart of the Universe,
Keeper of Time and Tides,
slow the tempo of her days
until all her time swells
rich with melody and meaning.
Let her feel the sweet space of every minute,
the symphonic expanse of an hour.
And let her dreams bloom with beautiful abandon
like birdsongs filling the blue Ohio sky
along the paths of our childhood,
when cancer was a word related to
others, but not to us,
when our only concern,
walking home from piano lessons,
was for the hour before us:
spending our bus money on ice cream
and singing all the way home
in harmony and innocence.

Karen Leahy, sixty, had written a poem after her father's death that her sister, Ginny, had framed for her home. Then, in October 1999, Ginny was diagnosed with an aggressive brain cancer — treatable, but not curable. When she heard about the Cancer Poetry Project, she asked Karen to write a poem for her.

"I felt a poem could honor her and our relationship," says Leahy. "But it did more than that: It helped me see just how rich our relationship has been." This is her first published poem.

Leahy, who now lives in Great Neck, New York, grew up in a large musical family in Ohio. She has taught English and music and worked for a nonprofit administration. Today she is pursuing her lifelong interests in writing, painting, and music, and has recently released a limited-edition CD.

GIVING THE DARKNESS SHAPE

by Laura Stearns

Toward nightfall, the cancer comes
for Grandfather's blood, his bones,
his face. Each hour, the nurses
turn his bedsored body toward
the sleep of white lilies, carnation
wreaths from Grandmother's church.
Grandfather is curled too tight
for a wheelchair, a ride down the hall.
He does not recognize my sister or me,
standing beside his bed like small angels.
"Rise," we want to say, "chatter
to us in mock Chinese, tell us
your headhunter stories, how you swam
back to the ship's belly in a rain of spears."

Our parents do not speak. This vigil
kept so long by the bedside,
in the dark lobby, all night next to the phone.
"If he knew it was cancer," Grandmother says,
"he would jump out the window. Your Uncle Clem,
Aunt Noreen and Pearl all dead." We drive back
to our grandparents' house, to Grandfather's
razor propped in the glass, his ribbed undershirts
draped on the drying rack in the tub.
"Pop won't die," Grandmother says, stirring
and stirring a deep crock of apricots on the stove.

My sister and I do not have any words.
Only the crude crosses for distempered kittens,
a banty who wandered the road.
Our parents sit on the sofa and watch the late news.
I carry the deck of cards to them.
Someone shuffles and the whole house stills.

When Laura Stearns' grandfather was diagnosed with advanced prostate cancer, the disease spread too quickly for treatment to be effective. "There is a place in my heart that still grieves for my much-beloved grandfather. This poem enables me to pay tribute to him and let him know that he is by no means forgotten," says Stearns, forty-three.

Stearns' work has been published in Boomer Girls: Poems by Women from the Baby Boom Generation *(University of Iowa Press, 1999),* Essential Love: Poems about Mothers, Fathers, Daughters, and Sons *(Grayson Books, 2000), and many literary magazines. She lives in San Francisco, California, where she contracts her writing services to Bay Area corporations.*

LET US NOW PRAISE

by Judith McCombs

the one stubbornly
out in the mid-
morning sun, raking his
leaves down the winter-
drained slope of his yard
to the curb, a shining
new walker set at his
right, and a white
metal chair from the kitchen
guarding his left:

and the one glimpsed
from a hallway, or hidden
by curtains, who day after
night after day, still
makes her good hand
catch hold of the gleaming
triangle that hangs
above her barred bed,
who grimacing lifts
a weight so precarious
three shifts of nurses
can't manage it safely.

Judith McCombs, sixty-two, wrote this poem several years after her mother's death from breast cancer. "I saw an old man raking leaves and admired him for that," she says. "And then I thought of my chin-up, determined mother and how much stubborn hoping and coping there is that one doesn't see."

McCombs has written three books of poetry, including Territories, Here and Elsewhere *(Mayapple Press, 1996). Her poems have also appeared in many journals and anthologies, including* Poetry, Calyx, *and* Nimrod. *She is the author of two books on Margaret Atwood and the founder of* Moving Out, *the nation's second-oldest surviving feminist literary journal.*

Retired from college and university teaching, McCombs writes as a poet and scholar and lives with her husband at the edge of a forest in Maryland.

PRACTICING MY GOODBYE AFTER HE'S GONE

by Jeffrey L. Stangl

Rolling over to say hello
Was a marathon event.
He was a bundle of pick-up sticks
Waiting for that precarious black one to be snatched
So that he could collapse, be gathered up neatly
And shelved.

I jabbered inanely to a weary traveler
About my travels which had taken me every direction but his.
He nodded. He knew.

Stopping mid-sentence, I took up his hand, his bony, long-fingered hand
That, not long ago, before the cancer announced itself, had gripped a paddle
And taught me to guide our not-invincible Kevlar canoe
Deftly through rocky rapids and around deadheads.
After a few moments he squeezed my hand hard,
Tighter than I would have imagined possible.

Words were obsolete,
As outmoded as his houseful of American Indian artifacts
Collected in a lifetime of study, love, and respect
For a spiritual way of life which consoled us now
Like nothing out of our genuflecting past could.

Everything I knew about saying goodbye
Was as shallow and grating
As the sandy-bottomed Chippewa River
We had so often scraped down
And assumed we'd all wake up tomorrow,
Disheveled, but safe inside the tent.

The timing of my goodbye
Is no worse than his.
Dammit.

Jeffrey L. Stangl, fifty-four, lost his father to colon cancer in April 1998, after a two-and-a-half-year battle. "I wrote this poem out of the loss and the help-lessness I felt," Stangl says. "Writing is one way I express my emotions, and poetry allows that more than anything else."

Stangl quit his job two years ago to pursue poetry and short story writing full time. He lives with his wife on the banks of the Mississippi in Buffalo City, Wisconsin. "The flow of the river is good for the spirit," he says. They have two grown children.

IN COLD DREAMS BEFORE DAWN

by Muriel Fish

where diagrammed pamphlets clinically
spell out precise directions for breast self-exams,
I fearfully imagine the snap of my doctor's rubber
gloves, preparing to press and rub my breasts,
searching for lumping, pebbling, dimpling, my
nipples hardening in protest, his gloves leaving
a powdery residue dusty against skin lovers have
brushed with their lips. A lump the size

of a pea is palpated on the outer left quadrant
in my left breast. The doctor orders a mammogram
and biopsy. A technician places my breasts
between cold sheets of glass where they become
splayed for the x-ray. It takes about fifteen
minutes but feels like an hour. Fear tastes sour
in my mouth. I crave a drink of water. The radiologist
enters, snaps the x-ray film into a wall unit lit with

brisk efficiency. I reach out, touching the mass with
cold fingertips. The bite of the biopsy needle reminds me
most lumps are benign. The nurse helps me into
my blouse, works the buttons because I'm trembling,
and hastens to call someone. I wait, remembering long
bittersweet days sitting with my mother and sister, each
with their own small malignancy and dead within three years.

Muriel Fish, forty-two, wrote this poem after a particularly moving conversation with a breast cancer survivor. As the former director of the MaineCares Women's Health Coalition, she daily encountered women dealing with breast cancer. This poem, written in the voice of her mother, describes a suspicious finding during a yearly mammogram. Making this finding especially scary was the fact that her mother is the only remaining sibling of ten children, all of whom have died from cancer.

Fish's poetry has appeared in such journals as Animus #4 *and* The Maine Literary Journal. *She also teaches creative writing. She and husband David live in Smithfield, Maine.*

AN EXPLANATION TO MY DYING DAUGHTER

by Francie Freeman

You say you do not understand
Why I sorrow for the loss of things
Rather than for the greater losses
Your time of travail brings.
Oh, my child, don't you know
That sometimes to endure we choose
To grieve for unimportant things
That we can bear to lose.

COURAGE
For my daughter during cancer treatment

by Francie Freeman

Each day she takes the sprig of rue
Death holds out to her and then
She tucks it into his own buttonhole
And reaches for life's flowers again.

Francie Freeman, seventy-six, was inspired to write poetry when her daughter was diagnosed with non-Hodgkin's lymphoma. "I write poems about what I'm thinking and feeling," Freeman says. Today her daughter is on a clinical trial.

A published poet, Freeman lives in Eden Prairie, Minnesota. She has two daughters and three grandchildren.

YAHRZEIT

by Dr. Bonnie Salomon

KILLER QUAKE ROCKS JAPAN
Screams the headline on page one.
Hundreds dead, smashed in rubble,
Families lost, homes destroyed.
Torrents of rain follow,
Mudslides flooding streets,
Overturning cars and shops.
Countless injured, fractured, or burned.
Survivors search for relatives
Lost under beams and stones.
A national emergency is called.
A world away, a different sort
Of catastrophe occurs:
I light your Yahrzeit candle,
A year to the day you left.
My soul smashed in the rubble,
Our family lost, our home destroyed.
Torrents of tears followed,
Anger flooding our hearts,
Overturning our reason and daily lives.
Countless pains, breaks with friends.
Survivors all, we searched for you
In the wind, on the beach, at your grave.
No national emergency was called.
Nature sweeps away masses with one tremor,
Or quietly grows a misguided cancer cell.
Results remain the same to those left
Standing beside the casket.
Natural disasters come in all forms:
The newspapers tell of one kind,
Your Yahrzeit candle tells of mine.

Dr. Bonnie Salomon, thirty-nine, wrote "Yahrzeit" on the first anniversary of her sister Jeanne's death from lung cancer. "I had read about an earthquake in Japan, and the enormity of my loss seemed to match the enormity of a natural disaster," Salomon says. "Part cheerleader, mentor, and girlfriend, Jeanne convinced me to become a doctor. I watched her die in the hospital where I worked." Yahrzeit is a Yiddish term for the anniversary of a death.

Salomon is an emergency-room physician who lives in the Chicago area with husband Michael and son Jonathan (named after Jeanne). Her poetry has appeared in a number of medical and literary journals.

WINDSTORM

by Larry Schug

In the eye of the night I lie awake,
half afraid, half in awe of the wind
penetrating every crack in my being.
I think of my brother and his wife
in the next town downwind,
open-eyed and clinging to each other
as the wind that mocks everything
to which we think we're anchored
roars through our lives.
I see them leaning in the gale;
how tightly they must be holding each other –
like roots gripping the soil,
as my brother's cancer blows away his time,
minutes flying off like shingles from a roof;
and I hear the cry in his wife's heart
drowning even the howling outside their walls.
I roll closer to my own wife this night,
circle her in my arms, desperately.

"I was moved to write this poem out of love and fear for my brother, Mike, and his wife, as well as for my wife and myself," says Larry Schug, fifty-four. He adds that many tears went into writing this poem. Mike was diagnosed with lung cancer four years ago, despite the fact that he hadn't smoked for nearly twenty years. "In fact, he ran marathons," Schug says. "He went through the usual chemo-radiation therapy, to no avail." His brother died within eight months.

Schug lives with his wife, two cats, and one dog near a large tamarack bog in St. Wendel Township, Minnesota. He has published four volumes of poems.

The Cancer Poetry Project

A MOTHER AND A DAUGHTER

by Elizabeth Ann Johnson

Mommy, when you were my mother
I held the look of you in my eyes
knowing I would never be so beautiful
and when I held you as my daughter
and rocked you to sleep
you asked me to rub the place on your belly
where the tumors were . . .
and you cried to me
but how will I live, how will I live?
You cursed yourself for weakness
And I blame you still for bad mothering

I remember what Joy smells like
on a Hermes scarf when you wore them
around your neck, not your head. And
I still open my refrigerator expecting a jar
of marinated artichoke hearts to be
waiting for me.

I can see us as we were back then –
me, a solemn seventeen with
ripped bleached jeans and a long
braid down my back –
you on the edge of the bed
sucking on the joint
turning away so our eyes couldn't meet.
It was much too late to protect me, Mommy
it was much too late.

In the hospital you begged me for more morphine
You pleaded for me to take the pain away –
Your voice as it screamed my name still haunts me
And I can still see us as we were back then –
A mother and a daughter grieving for the other.

RED

by Elizabeth Ann Johnson

You and I
like two laughing girls
hung over the banister and
watched . . .

big stupid grins on our faces,
big red curls falling through
the spaces between the wood.

We had pulled them out in handfuls,
big beautiful red spirals that swung
'round your freckled face
that danced across the green in your eyes.

it was a chemo ago –
or two
maybe three

Maybe a world's gone by
since your hair looped
and flip-flopped and criss-
crossed the crossroads
of my young life.

Now I kiss the empty
space, the bald space
the lonely space
the death white silence
the graveyard of red
roots

We had pulled them out
in handfuls
big beautiful
red spirals
and watched them sail
through that warm
spring wind
and paint
the sky red with the
color of your life.

Elizabeth Ann Johnson, now twenty-nine, started writing poetry about her mother's ovarian cancer when she was twelve years old. Five years later, her mother, Darryle Lesh, died. Johnson wrote "Red" the following year.

"Cancer opened me up to writing poetry," she says. "Now I write about positive things, too." Johnson had kept her poetry to herself until submitting it to the Cancer Poetry Project; these are her first published poems. She lives in Antigo, Wisconsin, where she trains and races forty sled dogs competitively.

THE MIRACLE OF MILKWEED

by Ross Klongerbo

The day he died,
cancer like the grip of winter
clenched his heart.
He was withered and dry like
a Minnesota milkweed,
shrunken and sallow,
desiccated, a dry husk
enfolding only emptiness,
light as a whisper.

Suddenly, an explosion:
a single milkweed pod
like the white blossom of a soul,
seeds bursting from the pod,
shooting outward and up,
feather-like catching the wind
and softly and swiftly
rising toward the stars,
white seeds of love
and remembrance casting themselves
away from the shell,
fluttering like heartbeats,
to find a fertile ground
in which to rest,
to burrow deep into the
warmth of the world once again,
to await a distant spring.

Ross Klongerbo, forty-eight, wrote this poem out of "love and grief and admiration," both for his father, who died of lung cancer in 1988, and for his mother, a two-time cancer survivor. Klongerbo's poetry has appeared in a number of publications, including English Journal *and* Lyrical Iowa.

Klongerbo has taught English and writing at the high-school and college level for twenty-three years. He lives with his wife of twenty-five years, Terri, and their two teenagers in Winter Park, Florida.

ON THE BEACH
For Mother

by Stephen J. Kudless

It was a shark, her disease.
It took her in many bites;
At first, in tiny nibbles –
bit
by
bit
Leaving scars and hope.
Then, the shark, roused by her blood
Became frenzied and bold –
Devouring, obliterating.
She thrashed and cried out,
In the crimson water,
And was gone.

Now the sea is quiet, even peaceful and blue.
The gulls wheel overhead
And the tiny crabs fiddle in the ebb tide.
They are oblivious to what I know.
Children make castles in the sand,
And parents make plans for dinner.

I see it, though, circling,
Its fin just creasing the surface
Out in the distance,
Just beyond the lifeguards' sight,
This shark, fed on motherflesh,
And still hungry.

I fear the water.

Stephen J. Kudless, sixty, often thinks of the courage of his mother, a surgical nurse and "an obstinate Irish woman," in the face of cancer. Diagnosed with breast cancer in 1983, she underwent a mastectomy and enjoyed five years of cancer-free living. After the cancer returned, she survived twelve more months before dying at age seventy-nine. He wrote "On the Beach" in her memory and because so many other people he knows have been diagnosed with cancer.

Kudless, a college English instructor, writes poetry, short stories, and non-fiction. He lives with his wife on Staten Island, New York. They have two grown children.

MAKING PIES IN THE DARK

by Elaine Wright Christensen

He could hear her in the kitchen
opening the fridge,
sounding shocked at how little
was left on the shelves.
Maybe she couldn't cook in heaven.
Maybe that's why he could hear
the heavy slide of the flour drawer opening,
a scoop ladling out one cup, then another,
the sifter's metal crank, turning quickly,
the sound of fork and knife cutting butter
into the flour in a glass bowl,
making pies in the dark.
She could do it, easily.

He coughed, turned over, hoping she'd come,
an angel to check on him.
But now the rolling pin thumps in one direction,
then another, across the breadboard.
He holds his breath.
The oven door opens, closes.
She sets the timer and is gone.

He never noticed how old the house was,
green shag carpet,
autumn gold stove,
till the day he came home
carrying one rose chosen from the coffin spray,
or how old *he* was,
her hospital bed still spelling the word *death*
in the living room.

Such a short word to live so long.
It thrives still in her closet, her dresser drawers,
clings in the folds of the floral drapes she made,
surprises him in the mailbox,
in the hedge turning lavender. He had no idea
lilacs could spell.

Tonight though, he sleeps, a young man,
peach juices in his veins,
lips stained strawberry rhubarb,
his favorite.

---

*Elaine Wright Christensen, fifty-two, raves about her mother-in-law's cooking.
"She would never make just one or two pies, always at least a dozen,"
Christensen says. "If she came back, it would be to cook for her husband."
Seeing her mother-in-law's house turn into a place of death as she battled
breast cancer, and then watching her father-in-law learn to cope there after
his wife's death, inspired Christensen to write this poem.*

*An award-winning poet, Christensen has had poems published in such
journals as* Weber Studies, The Ensign, Dialogue, *and* Ellipsis. *Her first
book,* At the Edges *(Utah State Poetry Contest, 1990), won the Pearle M.
Olsen Book Award sponsored by the Utah State Poetry Society. Her second,* I
Have Learned Five Things *(Lake Shore Publishing, 1996), won the
National Federation of Poetry Societies' Stevens Manuscript Contest.*

*An army brat, Christensen grew up in Japan, Germany, and the United
States. She now lives with her husband in Sandy, Utah. She is the mother of
five children.*

CHRYSALIS

by Brian Long

The film is dark
in his hands, rumbles
when he tips it toward the light –
strange, warped thunders.

It is a sentence:
This is the cancer,
and he points to the spot
with a gnawed red pen.
Something hangs deep at her center.

Options are given, odds
are placed in careful scale, weighed,
and he excuses himself
so she may tremble.

She touches a screen of bone and shadow,
flat, cold, antiseptic.
There is nothing to feel.

In the waiting room the family is patient,
still as willows in slow August rains.
Her voice is a wind that shakes tears from limbs;
they stand,
sway,
bend.

Evening, and she sits on the porch swing.
Moths beat at the streetlamps.
The light hums.
She listens close so she may know the sound
when, and soon, the night
will be cool beneath the dust
of new and sudden wings.

When Brian Long, now thirty-one, was barely three years old, his father was killed in an automobile accident. His grandmother became very involved in his upbringing. "She took great care to make sure I knew my father, though I could not remember more than stray moments with him," he says.

His close relationship with his grandmother caused him to "go through the list of emotions when she was diagnosed with cancer," Long says. "In truth, she was much stronger than I was. Perhaps this poem was a way for me to make my fear into something tangible, a 'made thing' that I could hold in my hands, rattle, crumple, throw away." She died July 27, 2000, at age seventy.

Other poems by Long have appeared in an anthology, The Vision *(Indian Heritage Publishing, 2000), and in such journals as* ByLine Magazine, Salonika, The Bible Advocate, *and* The MAPP.

Long, a hotel manager, lives in Knoxville, Tennessee, with his wife of thirteen years – "my first and only love" – and an eight-year-old son.

AGAIN, JULY
For Alice (July 2, 1939, to July 7, 1989)

by Kathleen Large

I want to place yellow roses –
never mind.

Exhaustion drains the day.
In private, there is solace.
But only in private.

Each year in July you are fifty.

Your husband has become grey-haired,
a writer instead of the engineer you knew.
I live in a city you have never seen.
There are few people who knew you, who know me.

Once in a while someone calls me by your name.
Once in a while you receive mail.

I want to draw you a map of how I have changed.
Is there a way to explain
your look on my face?

The body remembers the body (only).

Only its gestures,
the way you carry yourself at a party
wearing a tailored white dress,
hair slicked back.

Of all the ways I miss you, this is the best.

The Cancer Poetry Project

The body is contagious.
Or so I thought –
As if planning death were prohibiting.

These ten years,
I have wondered over seeing
my father's naked body on your bed
after the funeral.

Perhaps it was the only way to say:
"There is nothing left."

Today,

I want to place yellow roses

in every corner of my grief

every space

it hollows.

Kathleen Large, thirty-one, started writing cancer-themed poetry after her mother died of breast cancer in 1989, twelve years after her original diagnosis. "I have never considered her a 'cancer patient' or 'cancer victim,' but a long-term survivor of cancer. She outlived her prognosis by years, and she was able to live a high-quality life both in between and during her bouts with cancer. She came back from her second diagnosis to run a marathon and start her own business, and she worked up until the week before she died.

"I wrote this poem on the fifth anniversary of her death," Large says, adding that her mother also had written poetry about her cancer. "Writing is my way of staying connected to her. If I did not have writing, I would have lost my mother long ago."

After living in New York for ten years, Large is back in her native California, in San Francisco, where she teaches high school English and writes poetry.

ONE LAST FAVOR

by Marilyn L. Taylor

Why yes,
there is something
you can do for us
before you die.
You can please quit
grieving. Stop

leaking out all over us
your sorrow and your
dread. It's hard
for us to watch,
we don't like it,

we would so much rather
have you smiling like
a picture of Saint Jude,
stroking our hands and
telling us *There there,*

this was to be expected.
But with your whole spine
gone bent like that and
your head shaking back
and forth, your eyelids

stiff with fear and every
wasted muscle straining
to deny, deny – just where
are we supposed to turn
for comfort now?

Marilyn L. Taylor, sixty-one, lost her mother in 1974 and her older sister in 1991, both to lung cancer. "Both women were strong, capable, and depended upon in times of crisis, not only for comfort, but for taking charge — 'doing the necessary,' as my mother would always put it," Taylor says. "So when they died, the rest of us were stymied; there was no one left to take on the 'rock of Gibraltar' role that they had both filled so gracefully."

Taylor is married and has one son in graduate school. She teaches poetry for the honors program at the University of Wisconsin, Milwaukee, where she earned her doctorate in 1991. Another poem by Taylor, "Leaving the Clinic," appears on page 196.

GARDEN VARIETY

by Colette Giles Tennant

1.

Still in impervious scrub blues, the doctor
described, in a too-chirpy voice,
my mother's lung cancer:
"garden variety."

Like spiders seeping through cracks
in cold weather.
(You don't know exactly how they get there.
You just know they can.)
This year my daughter and I each
adopted one as a pet.

Hers caught her attention when it
feigned injury, tucking two legs under its body,
hoping to look dead – or fatally maimed.

Mine lived behind an Oscar de la Renta perfume bottle
on my bathroom vanity,
every morning sitting there well-mannered,
watching me put on makeup.

2.

But one day
I looked in the mirror
and discovered her dangling
right next to my cheek.
I grabbed the first hardbound book
I could find and that was that.

I don't know really if the doctor chose his words well,
meant "garden variety" cancer or "garden variety" patient,
but I do know that all of my friends
in this garden of second chances
dance between the ceiling and a hardbound book.

---

*Colette Giles Tennant, forty-eight, was present when a surgeon nonchalantly
called her mother's lung cancer the "garden variety" type. "Writing about can-
cer helped me deal with the stress of those months," she says. "I lost my father
to lung cancer when I was fourteen, and all of that pain had come back."*

*Tennant, herself a skin cancer survivor, has had her poetry included in
various journals and anthologies, including* Entre Nous *and* Nostalgia.
"Garden Variety" first appeared in the 2000 issue of The Anthology of
New England Writers. *Her poem "Petals on the Ground" became the text
for a musical piece that memorializes the tragedy at Columbine High
School in Colorado.*

*Tennant lives with her husband of twenty-seven years, Stuart, in Salem,
Oregon, where she is a professor of English and humanities at Western Baptist
College. They have three children: Shannon, Jeremy, and Andrew.*

PERSEPHONE
For Vanessa

by Janine Soucie Kelley

It is winter. Christmas.
And you are half-asleep
from the terrible drugs
with mysterious Latin
and Greek names riding
through your veins – one
means place of death.
Like half-mad Demeter,
I grieve for a daughter lost
in hell. Thirteen.
This was to be the season
of your first dance, a first
kiss – but cancer like a wolf
has come howling to your bed.
The sun is dark, all
innocence lost, and life
more cruel than any legend.

I wait and pray, the stars
small covenants of light.
From the hospital window,
we watch the sky.
It is snowing. The first snow.
Nurses, pale angels, come and go
to take your pulse,
to count your blood,
to anchor your arms to more machines.
Like Christ, you say nothing.
I touch your face, your shaven head,
and trace the soul beneath your skin.
You smile. I whisper carols

in your ear, promises
of Bethlehem and kings, an end
to this mad myth, spring.

Janine Soucie Kelley, fifty, says she was moved to write this poem by "my daughter's anguish, and by my connection with other mothers who have witnessed the loss of innocence in their children." Her daughter, Vanessa, was diagnosed with a rare form of ovarian cancer at age thirteen. "Grief and rage at the thought of losing a beloved child, at her suffering, seemed at times like an endless winter. But in the midst of this terrible suffering, I found hope in the enduring love, the abiding compassion of family and friends. Just as a poem ends, so too does cancer and its terrible suffering. Cancer is a season in a family's life. With the faith and love of community, the family is restored to hope, to spring." Today, Vanessa has been cancer free for seven years, and at age twenty "she has parachuted into acting in Portland, Oregon."

The former editor of Southwest Literary Magazine, *Kelley is writing her first novel, as well as a family memoir. She lives in Flagstaff, Arizona, with husband John, who is a musician and mechanic, and son Brandon, who hopes to be his generation's George Lucas.*

SHARING

by Sam Friedman

I have joined my daughter in a new language,
feelings,
tastes:
the slicing of the biopsy blade,
sipping barium sulfate,
nervous ounce after nervous ounces,
iodine flickering metallic on empty tongues,
the horizontal dance through the doughnut
as the CAT scans intestines, vessels, fates.

We have each been invited to the ball
by the big empty.
We have each stepped back for the nonce,
back from that dance, from the lilting tempos
of Mr. Bones.

Sam Friedman, fifty-eight, was diagnosed with testicular teratoma four years ago. It was surgically removed, and his CAT scans have been clear ever since. Meanwhile, his daughter, Catherine, was diagnosed with disseminated Hodgkin's disease and went through a difficult course of chemotherapy. "One night I woke up with the concept for this poem in my head," Friedman explains. Now Catherine, too, is doing well; and she is attending medical school.

Poems by Friedman have appeared in a number of journals, including Canadian Dimension, Home Planet News *and* Longshot. *His chapbook is called* Needles, Drugs, and Defiance: Poems to Organize By *(North American Syringe Exchange Network, 1999).*

Friedman works as an AIDS researcher in New York City. He lives with wife Judy in Highland Park, New Jersey.

POEMS BY FRIENDS AND HEALTH ADVISORS

THE WRONG MONTH
For Bob DuRard

by Anthony Russell White

This cannot be real rain
this is not a rainmonth
some kind of heavy fog, not really rain

This cannot be real crab
this is not a crabmonth
something made to look like fresh crab

You cannot really be dying
this is not a dyingmonth
some terrible mistake has been made

Anthony Russell White, sixty-two, and Bob DuRard were best friends for twenty years. In 1996, they went on a retreat together at Christ-in-the-Desert Monastery, near Abiquiu, New Mexico. "Although I wrote a number of poems there, this one was written shortly after our return to California," White says. *"A month later, Bob was diagnosed with cancers of the stomach, liver, and pancreas. I don't know where the poem came from; I didn't know that he was ill at the time. He died three years later, close to his sixty-first birthday. I miss him terribly."*

White's "New Year's Poem, 1998" won the 1999 Rainer Maria Rilke International Competition and was published in Artlife. *His latest chapbook,* How I Learned about Baseball *(Talent House Press, 2000), includes "The Wrong Month," to which White added the dedication that he read at DuRard's funeral.*

White is a new grandfather and lives on a mountaintop in San Rafael, California, with his poet wife, Daphne Crocker-White. He devotes much of his time to staffing the Nine Gates Mystery School four times a year.

THE DIAGNOSIS

by Majid Mohiuddin

He opens the door
      and walks in,
his face and white coat
stiff with starch,

holds my hand, and
he says
"I'm afraid.

I am afraid
you have cancer."

Cancer.
The words come out
as if the doctor himself were
coughing up blood.

In my mind grows cancer.

Cancer
I can't
      can
      surly and ugly
callous

cancel
Kansir?

If I clicked my heels, three times,
I might wake up again
in Kansas.

"In this poem, I wanted to describe the initial impact that a cancer diagnosis has on a patient, as well as the role the physician plays at that moment," says Majid Mohiuddin, twenty-five. "Many of my poems are inspired by my interaction with oncology patients. I often use these poems to encourage other patients who are undergoing various stages of treatment. These patients are part of my 'family,' and they seem to appreciate my words."

In May 2000, "The Diagnosis" won first place in a creative writing contest sponsored by the Society of General Internal Medicine. The poem first appeared in The Journal of General Internal Medicine. *Mohiuddin has also published creative works about Islam and spirituality.*

The son of an oncologist, Mohiuddin is a medical student at Brown University and will soon begin his residency in radiation oncology.

AWKWARD FRIENDS

by Laurel Winter

I don't want to act like everything's different –
    it isn't
    you are still the you I know

I don't want to act like everything's the same –
    it isn't
    you're dancing too close with this disease

I don't know what to do, or what to say
but I don't want the fear of saying something stupid
to stop me from saying anything –
    such a small fear
    compared to your fears –
I haven't even mentioned the D word.

Does it drive you crazy, make you tired
when the phone keeps ringing?
    Or does it give you a sense of connection?
Do you get tired of explaining the diagnosis,
the prognosis, the not-so-hot odds?
    Or does it help, not being the only one who knows?

I can bring chocolate (the drug of choice)
    give rides
    lend you positive mental attitude books
    give hugs
    talk about regular stuff
        (which books are or aren't worth reading,
        Godiva chocolate vs. Hershey's,
        Henry David Thoreau)
    talk about the other stuff
        (anger, fear, disease)

You're probably not any better
at knowing how to deal with awkward friends
than I am at being one,
but I'm willing if you are.
             Let me know when I do something stupid.

Laurel Winter, forty-two, was a member of the same writers group as her friend, L. A. Taylor, when Taylor was diagnosed with cancer. "She was a science fiction writer, poet, artist, singer, and good friend," Winter says. "It was difficult to see her brain tumor rob her slowly of her coordination, her creativity, and her life. I gave her a copy of the poem, and she and her family greatly appreciated it." Winter also read the poem at Taylor's funeral.

Winter's poetry has appeared in numerous publications, primarily in science fiction and fantasy magazines. She won both the Asimov's Reader Poll Award for best poem and the Rhysling Award of the Science Fiction Poetry Association two years in a row. Her first novel, Growing Wings *(Houghton Mifflin), was published in 2000.*

Winter grew up in the mountains of Montana and now lives in a passive-solar, earth-bermed house in Rochester, Minnesota, with her husband and twin teenage sons.

SHE ASKED FOR A JOKE OR POEM

by Charles Rossiter

She could be cured
by the time I write a poem
so I send the joke
which is about chemotherapy
and not very funny,
and I tell her
I'll still love her
without hair,
it will be all right,
and to me she is still the Ava Gardner
in "Night of the Iguana"
who lights up all of Richard Burton's
Mexico.

Now I am thinking
of parties long ago,
like the night Jack scribbled
"I love Allen Ginsberg –
let that be recorded
in heaven's unchangeable
heart –"
        and now Jack's dead

or the night we played pool
and drank beer for hours
after hours of champagne,

the rest gone home,
stood in the driveway
and missed the dawn.
        Ava Gardner, I tell her

It will be all right.

The Cancer Poetry Project

*Charles Rossiter, fifty-eight, wrote this poem for friend and colleague Ruth
McGaffey at the University of Wisconsin, Milwaukee, following McGaffey's
diagnosis with cancer.* "One year, my wife and I flew back to visit Ruth and
her husband, Jeri, for their traditional New Year's Day party. Ruth had
already begun her fight with cancer, and things were going pretty well. At the
time, I deeply wanted to believe that everything would be all right. She fought
for years using the entire battery of weapons available to modern medicine,
but finally the cancer won."

"She Asked for a Poem or Joke" first appeared in the Journal of Poetry
Therapy. *"At the time it was written," Rossiter says, "Kerouac was dead, but
Ginsberg was still with us."*

*Rossiter, who has received a National Endowment for the Arts fellowship
for poetry and has been nominated for a Pushcart Prize, is a poet, grant
writer, and at-home dad who lives in Oak Park, Illinois, just outside of
Chicago. He also operates an audio web site,* www.poetrypoetry.com.

MY FRIEND

by Joanne Bergbom

Please, please don't let her
shudder
when I give her the lock of my hair,
or wince when she
recognizes my new look
is a wig.
Let her be able to say
with me
the words *cancer* and *die,*
and not retreat into
"You'll be just fine,"
or
"That's a style you should have tried
years ago."
Let us cry together,
tissueless,
until we laugh
at how absurd
our puffy-eyed faces look
cheek to courageous cheek.

"A close friend brought me a lock of her hair after beginning chemo for non-Hodgkin's lymphoma," says Joanne Bergbom, fifty-seven. "At that moment, I realized just how insignificant some of our daily worries can be. This was her message and her gift to me. Since then, whenever I feel discouraged, I look at the lock of hair and try to put everything in perspective." Today, her friend is cancer free. This is Bergbom's first published poem.

Bergbom, who lost her father to cancer when she was thirteen, is an English teacher at H. Frank Carey High School in Franklin Square, New York, where she has taught for seventeen years. She lives with husband Bruce in Garden City Park, Long Island, New York. She has two sons, two daughters, and two grandchildren.

SAY YES

by Marc J. Straus

If I cut down on fatty foods, lose
fifteen pounds, work out three times
a week, will I avoid a heart attack?

If only every question were that simple.
It's an opportunity to answer unequivocally,
to give patients a sense of purpose

and hope, even if they've always been obese,
refractory to treatment, unable to comply
with a regimen. Still, just to say yes

is palliative, even though they know
the answer isn't accurate. They don't want
to hear statistics and vacillation.

Just to be like the surgeon who says,
It's 100% curable – I got it all, omitting
the possibility that a cell, a micro-

metastasis, may already be elsewhere.
Say yes – a sliver of grace in an
excoriated world. I must try it sometime.

ROCKY ROAD

by Marc J. Straus

I suddenly have a craving for Chinese oolong tea.
For Mrs. Sudbury down the hall it is ice cream.
This I relate to easily. When my mother was ill
and lost forty pounds (though still not skinny by any means),
she was admonished to take in more nourishment.
All her life she craved ice cream but now a cholesterol of 350
was forgiven. The creamier the better. Cherry Garcia,
Chocolate Marshmallow Swirl, Oreo Cookie Crunch –
just the names brought her rapture. Doctor Donovan says
I can have strawberry milkshakes for breakfast.
Forget lamb chops. They taste like tires. Bring me
a large bowl of Rocky Road topped with Reese's Pieces
and a midnight snack of Double Rich Black Forest seven-layer cake
with lots of almonds. Oh, it is almost worth being sick
if we can indulge in that forbidden thing we most crave
without guilt: delicious, foolish and obscenely rich.

Marc J. Straus, fifty-seven, who runs an oncology practice in White Plains,
New York, began writing poetry in 1990 after attending a poetry class. Ten
years later, he has a number of literary awards and publications under his belt.

"I'm really compelled by the nuances in patient-doctor communication –
what it is that a doctor says and how it is received and internalized by the
patient," Straus told The New York Times *in June 2000. "In my world, I've*
[told] thousands of people for the very first time that they have cancer. I try
my best to absorb some of their anxiety by working really hard to support
them. You have to learn to hear your patients. It's not just the exact words you
say. It's how you say it.

"In some ways, 'Say Yes' is a personal poem. Patients ply us with questions
all the time. Sometimes they expect certain answers. Patients always want to
hear that what they have is 100 percent curable. They know that may not be
correct, but they really want an absolute answer. I think doctors do a disser-
vice to patients when we give them absolutes. So how you choose your words is
very important."

Straus' newest collection, Symmetry *(Northwestern University Press,*
2000), which includes "Say Yes," is being used in various medical school
ethics curricula. "Rocky Road" is part of a series of twenty-five poems, "The
Bridge," which was written in the voice of a fictional female patient; it had
its stage premiere at SUNY Purchase, New York, in April 2000.

Straus lives with wife Livia, a theologian who teaches medical ethics at
Fordham University.

DOUBLE MASTECTOMY

by Ann Campanella

This morning oats slide from the scoop like salmon
into the buckets of muttering horses.
I think of you prone on the table.

I climb the wooden ladder to the loft,
part the hay with my fingers, let it drop
from above into each stall.

I descend and toss last night's water to the ground like a prayer,
refill buckets with the smack of liquid hitting plastic.
You said it was nothing, this stupid little lump.

I sift under, around horses through curls of wood
for brown eggs of manure scattered during the night,
my pitchfork catches on the oak wall.

I open stall doors, hear the clatter of hooves on cement;
in the pasture their shoes slice even half-moons in the mud.
By noon your breasts will be gone

and still I have chores. I grab
the sharp bristled brush, overturn the trough
and try to scrub out the green slime.

I shake lime over urine-soaked bedding,
reach for the broom, lean into it and push stray shavings
across rough grooves of cement.

I wish you could be here tonight
to see that some things don't change.
The horses, as always, will hurry hungry down the hill,

file into the barn, nose to rump,
staining the white aisle with clods of mud
in the shape of crescents.

Ann Campanella, forty, was the 1999 poet laureate of North Carolina. She wrote "Double Mastectomy" after learning about her best friend's breast cancer. "Lyn and I bonded after spending a summer taking care of horses for our college's riding program," Campanella says. "Our friendship deepened over the years as we traveled to Europe, trained thoroughbreds in Texas, and wrangled mustangs in Wyoming. Horses communicate without language, and Lyn and I developed a similar kind of intuition. When I first learned her news, I was in shock, then I went through a period of deep grief. The idea that my dear friend might die was more than I could handle. I wrote a series of poems in an effort to deal with my raw emotion. This poem was written the day of Lyn's surgery." Today, Lyn is doing well.

"Double Mastectomy" won the Poetry of Courage Award from the North Carolina Poetry Society in 1998. Campanella's collection of poetry, Outrunning the Rain, *is forthcoming from Mount Olive College Press. She currently has a memoir under consideration with a publisher.*

Campanella writes poetry, fiction, and creative nonfiction. She lives on a small horse farm in Huntersville, North Carolina, with her husband, their horses, and their three cats.

THE DOOR

by David H. Huffman, MD

The door seems impenetrable.

Today is arduous.
I have seen patients with cancers of pancreas,
Gastric, cervix, colon – all unresectable.

One person with pancreas cancer
Fills my conscious: young and dying despite
His expectations and prayers.
I must be realistic, yet not hopeless.
Yet hope for what?
He doesn't understand why he's forty and dealing with this beast.

For balance, I try to remember the exhilaration of a patient cured.
I can only be forthright and compassionate.

Why is it so difficult to enter this room?
Maybe someday I will be in that bed.

I hope if that time comes
My doctor will be as truthful and considerate.

But if she hesitates at the door . . .
I will understand.

Dr. David H. Huffman, sixty, has worked as an oncologist for thirty years, the last twenty in Colorado. "Cancer care is a complicated life," he says. "Writing poetry and short stories about my work helps me to reconcile my feelings, it allows me to cope and express myself. I hope it also helps me to be a more sensitive, caring person and to get in touch with my patients' feelings." This is his first poem to be published in a national publication.

A native of Kansas, Huffman trained at Johns Hopkins and the National Cancer Institute. He is the father of seven children. He and wife Carol live in Colorado Springs.

PESACH

by Elizabeth Rosner

Already the angel of death is passing over
your house – door marked with the
bloody sacrifice, windows sealed
against the hovering plagues. The closeness
of beating wings demands your attention.
You say "I need to be
transformed" and so you are –
re-sculpted in the flesh,
scars wrapping you like a
talisman against the evil eye.
This must be
the narrow place you are
passing through: to be reborn
as one who knows the sound of
a silent warning overhead,
who knows the wounded body
can be carried into battle
with perfect beauty,
more holy, more whole.

Elizabeth Rosner, forty-one, wrote "Pesach" for her college friend, Lauren, who is currently experiencing a recurrence of breast cancer after having had a mastectomy five years ago. "I wrote the poem on the plane after visiting Lauren while she was going through chemotherapy," Rosner says. "I felt awed by the intensity of her ordeal, and at the same time I was deeply moved by her courage. The Passover holiday was approaching, and I suddenly realized the appropriateness of the symbolism: cancer as a journey or passage into a different kind of freedom. Now my mother is battling breast cancer, too, so the poem is doubly meaningful for me."

While her poetry has been published in a number of literary journals and anthologies, Rosner is also a novelist. Her first novel, The Speed of Light, *is due out in September 2001 from Ballantine Books.*

Rosner lives in Berkeley, California, where she teaches writing at a community college and is working on her second novel.

LEAVING THE CLINIC
Baja, California, 1997

by Marilyn L. Taylor

Carrying your own
terrible frailness
to the edge of the water

you bend your body sharply
like a broken stick, until
you are kneeling in the sand.

If the world weren't so damned
beautiful, you say, *maybe*
dying wouldn't be so bad –

But then you see how a small rain
has pocked the creamy skin
of the beach overnight

causing snails to leave their sanctuaries,
and the pursed hibiscus buds
to fatten and explode,

and with the sea collapsing around us,
thinning to a glassy sheen
that blinds you

you hide your face
behind your hands and shake
with unrequited love.

Marilyn L. Taylor, sixty-one, wrote "Leaving the Clinic" for a friend and local poet who had been to Mexico for cancer treatment, but who returned without much hope that she had been cured. "Her reaction involved not so much fear or anger, but sorrow at being forced to realize that she would soon have to give up the world around her, and all of its ordinary, everyday gorgeousness."

Taylor is married and has one son in graduate school. She teaches poetry for the honors program at the University of Wisconsin, Milwaukee, where she earned her doctorate in 1991. Another poem by Taylor, "One Last Favor," appears on page 170.

SEED

by Floyd Skloot

She is alive. Although her doctors said
there was nothing to be done, she is home,
planting her summer garden, is not dead,
and plans to eat everything she has grown
in this plot, each carrot and tomato,
each squash, pepper, lettuce leaf. She will live
beyond the harvest and what will not grow
is her tumor, its flowers held captive
and still beneath her heart. Only the live
wire of her will separates her now from
the future displayed in black and white five
months ago, backlit clearly. It will come
sooner or later, but this is her time
to cultivate and seed. She is alive.

IN REMISSION

by Floyd Skloot

This is a spring he never thought to see.
Lean dusky Alaskan geese nibbling grass
seed in his field, early daffodils, three
fawns moving across his lawn in the last
of afternoon light, everything he had
let go with small ceremonies on dark
September nights has suddenly come back.
The taste on his tongue is of tamarind
chutney, fish curry, clove, tangs he adores
above all else. He smells the hyacinth
and can feel hope with the terrible crack
of a thawing river loosen in his heart.
He imagines sailing among the Queen
Charlottes come April, tacking into wind
that is the kindest he has ever known,
then gentle breakers, golden sanded shores.

Floyd Skloot, fifty-three, wrote these poems out of his "love for two friends, and for their courage and determination to live meaningfully."

Skloot lives with wife Beverly in a small round house that she built on her twenty acres of forest in western Oregon. Disabled for twelve years, Skloot says the tranquil setting helps him to heal and work. His books include The Open Door *(Story Line Press, 1997) and* The Evening Light *(Story Line Press, 2001). His writings about illness appear in* The Best American Essays 2000 *(Houghton Mifflin) and* The Best American Science Writing 2000 *(Ecco Press).*

TO A FRIEND NOW SEPARATED FROM ME BY ILLNESS

by Gretchen Fletcher

Our lives until so recently
parallel and filled
with common details
once thought boring,
now precious –
paying phone bills
watering ferns
picking up car pools
dropping off dry cleaning –
details still in my life
while you lie in an alien bed,
your life now filled with details
I don't know, tubes and shunts
and treatments tried and failed.
I want to speak; you want to speak,
but we've lost our common language.
You've learned a new vocabulary
I don't know. How can I know
how it feels to lose a breast
and fight to save lungs,
bones, and brain
when all I have to battle
is the traffic?

Gretchen Fletcher, sixty, wrote this poem about a friend and fellow teacher.
"When I heard of her breast cancer and lengthy treatment, I was so shocked –
she was in her late thirties when diagnosed – that the only way I could
attempt to grasp the reality of her illness was through writing about it, trying
to express the horror in words."

Besides teaching fifth grade, Fletcher leads writing workshops in poetry
and personal essay for Florida Center for the Book. Her work has appeared in
such publications as Inkwell, Appalachian Heritage, *and* Pacific Coast
Journal. *She has two grown sons, one of whom also writes poetry.*

DINNER PARTY

by Susan Steger Welsh

We settle on Friday, her best day,
right after treatment but before it kicks in.
I cook without restraint, no regard
for cost or calories. For the soup,
the best mushrooms I can find –
Porcini, Portobello – real cream, the white
of a leek. A beef tenderloin, twice as big
as we need because she says, *I don't know why,*
but beef goes down so easy. Spinach
with artichokes and onion, sour cream
and Parmesan. Potato pancakes
made with apple and cheese. Popovers,
more butter – anything to fatten her up.
She alternately shivers and fans herself,
a disconcerting side effect, but her hair
is already coming back in,
like new grass. *Like a kitten,*
my husband exclaims when he touches it,
and she smiles as her husband
tells how their daughter likes to pet it
when they're driving. We talk
of new gutters, the warm fall,
a third-floor renovation going on
up the street. Nineteen years
of dinner parties all tumble
to this meal, this table, the four of us.
I have the urge to take their picture
but don't.

Susan Steger Welsh, now forty-six, was twenty-two years old when her mother died of cancer. Since then, she has seen too many people battle the disease. She wrote "Dinner Party" for a close friend who died on May 13, 2000, exactly one year after her cancer diagnosis and the day before Mother's Day. Rafting on the Water Table *(New Rivers Press, 2000) is her newest collection.*

A freelance writer, Steger Welsh lives with her husband and two children in a ninety-year-old house in St. Paul, Minnesota.

WHEN AUTUMN CAME

by Deborah Gordon Cooper

When I told her
on that morning
in the hospital
how beautiful she was,
lit from the inside,
she whispered back,
"I only became beautiful
when I began to die."

At the time, I didn't understand
her words and thought
it was the morphine.

Then, when autumn came,
I knew.
Seeing the trees along the road
release the fullness of
their radiance
all at once,
burning and shining
up and down the hills,
holding nothing back.

Deborah Cooper, fifty-one, has worked for twenty years as a chaplain, spending the past ten years at St. Mary's Hospice Program in Duluth, Minnesota. "I started writing poetry twelve years ago," she says. "I had to have some kind of ritual to let go of my work." Today, she encourages patients and their families to write poetry, and she conducts regular workshops on poetry and spirituality.

Cooper's work has been published in a number of literary journals and anthologies, including North Coast Review, Rag Mag, Loonfeather, *and* Kalliope. *She lives with husband Joel, a fine-art screen printer with whom she has exhibited her work. They have three grown children.*

THE WIDOW SPEAKS

by John Manesis

Doctor, thank you
for taking care of my husband.
We trusted you and understood
whatever could be done was done.
You did explain the chemotherapy,
detailed the possible side effects,
discussed survival rates –
so professional, so complete.
I'm sure that everything
you said was true,
but isn't there a way that you
can tell a man that he is dying
and still leave him with hope?

John Manesis, sixty-four, is a retired physician whose conversation with a widow over thirty years ago has always stayed with him. "My patient's wife spoke to me about his death, not in these exact words, but her message, so suc-cinctly stated, resonated with me and changed how I spoke with other patients."

Since retiring from medicine, Manesis has devoted much of his time to writing. "It's been wonderful for me," he says, "like a second career." His poems have been published in Wisconsin Review, California State Poetry Quarterly, Mediphors, *and* Zone 3. *He has a chapbook forthcoming.*

Manesis lives in Fargo, North Dakota, with wife Bess. They have four grown children.

THERE IS A WOMAN FALLING
For Robin, Matt, Brittany, and Brooke

by Karen Haas-Howland

There is a woman falling
    with the leaves.
She is brilliant, crimson, story-gold, and dying.

She is a forest of feelings, of color, of questions, of dreams
    crushed orange, cranberry rushing, wishing for more time
    time vital for love.

Like a leaf trying to understand the Northern wind's purpose,
    she is taken into circles
      slow and mysterious and fast.
Her name becomes the hush of maples,
    the holiness of oaks,
      the mist within willows.
The trees give her a strength
    telling her how to let go
    while remaining rooted to the embrace.
She remembers green
    remembers being three, then thirteen,
    then twenty, then thirty
    the years burn within her, a hearth
as the man she loved more than any other, gathers by her heart
    warming his hands, warming hers
    four gentle leaves meeting, touching, and parting.

Beautiful in their reach, beautiful in their ability to hold love
    even after it falls early, scarlet to the earth.
    Beautiful in their belief

    that certain birds, with fiery red breasts always return.

Karen Haas-Howland, thirty-six, had known Robin for many years when she realized that her friend would not survive breast cancer, despite a five-year battle. "I wrote this poem for my friend, with great emotion and with all I had learned while working on my master's degree in creative writing," she says.

A participant and facilitator of a women's writing circle, Haas-Howland has led the group in publishing two anthologies: Sparkle, Sizzle, Hiss *(1999) and* Womanifestos *(2000), both published by Moon Coo Press. Previously, she served as poetry editor for* Cream City Review.

Haas-Howland lives with her husband and two children in Milwaukee, Wisconsin.

I DID NOT KNOW HIS NAME

by Terri S. Hudson

I did not know his name
but he held out his hand.
I held it.

I did not know his name
but he asked to be held.
I held him.

I did not know his name
but he needed his brow wiped.
I washed his face.

I did not know his name
but he needed someone.
I sat with him.

I did not know his name
but he was frightened.
I comforted him.

I did not know his name
and then he was gone.

His name was John.

Terri S. Hudson, thirty-eight, is a social worker on the oncology floor at a hospital. When she realized that no one was visiting an aggressive patient who had cancer, she decided to make him a priority. "He needed someone to talk with him about dying," she says. "The floor was so busy that day that I honestly didn't know his name. I became his family for the next two days so he could pass more easily."

While Hudson writes poetry for her partner and children, "I did not know his name" is her first published poem, kept under her ink blotter at work for three years until submitted to the Cancer Poetry Project.

Hudson lives with her partner, Lisa, and their two children, Emily and Elijah, in Canton, Ohio, where she works for Aultman Hospice.

FOR LORRAINE

by Dr. Nelson L. Rhodus

A mere wisp of an old woman . . .
    Hovering . . .
    all about in her walker. Beaming,
        when I first met her and thereafter.

    Even then,
        almost an angel.   YET,

        suffering . . .
            beneath the surface.

    My heart reaches.

She reminds me of a little
starfish,

        found on a lonely beach of my youth . . .
        delicate, fragile, lovely, that

I thoughtfully packed in Kleenex for
    the hazardous journey home.

Despite my conscientious care, it still
    shattered . . .
        into a hundred pieces. A sad

    transition
            but now fully . . .

        an angel.

"Lorraine Schabel was a cancer patient whom I treated for two to three years," says Dr. Nelson L. Rhodus, who serves as the director of oral medicine, diagnosis, and radiology at the University of Minnesota. "Lorraine was elderly and had to use a walker. But she always was cheerful, bright, and friendly, and she didn't let her condition get her down. She was an inspiration." Lorraine reminded Rhodus of his own mother, who died in 1997.

Encouraged by his mother to write poetry at an early age, Rhodus often writes about his personal relationships with his patients. He has had a number of poems published.

While Rhodus grew up in Kentucky, he currently lives in St. Paul, Minnesota, with his wife of twenty-three years, Patti, and their three children: Nelson, twenty; Brianne, seventeen; and Evan, fourteen.

THEOLOGY

by Sima Rabinowitz

The language for speaking to and about God is metaphoric,
says the feminist Talmudic scholar.
I'd be interested in a more direct approach myself,
though I have to say I can understand
the appeal of speaking in tongues,
consonants glued together like oatmeal or aspic,
sticky and thick with confidence,
no place for puns, or analogies, or parody,
so utterly illogical, they're believable –
                              – or, at least, indisputable.

God's name is God,
says a little girl to her mother in the coffee shop on 54th and Lyndale.
It's directness I crave, yes, specificity, some granite evidence
when you tell me, dead metaphor:
                    It's the size of a grapefruit.
                    I'll have to do another round of chemo.

Not something or someone to accuse necessarily,
but a name less precise and more accurate,
a way to call attention to the rock solid face of grief.

Sima Rabinowitz, forty-four, was working on a series of poems with Jewish themes when one of her closest friends was diagnosed with liposarcoma. "Many of the poems in this series consider the relationship between the metaphorical and the literal. In this poem, I wanted to explore what it means to 'know' something (the meaning of God, or the size or location or toxicity of a tumor) precisely and to relay that knowledge as fact, as emotion, as concrete and abstract reality." Rabinowitz is happy to report that her friend is now cancer free.

Rabinowitz's writing has appeared in a variety of publications including Witness, Minnesota Monthly, *and* The Chiron Review. *She lives in Minneapolis, Minnesota, with her partner, Susan, and two extraordinary cats, Greta and Cecile, rescued from life on the streets.*

UNTITLED

by B. A. (Bonnie) St. Andrews

She hates that phrase "lost breast"
with its insinuation of carelessness.
"It's not as if the three of us went off
to market," she says, "my left breast,
my right breast and I, and one zipped off
to ice cream while the other darted to
bottled dressings and me just meandering
beside vegetables stacked and clotted
like a painter's palette with apricot,
celeriac, eggplant, muscadine. It's not
as if I realized suddenly one of my breasts
had gone missing and charged the courtesy
counter breathless on the PA system
announcing: "I'm waiting on aisle nine
for my right breast, my recalcitrant child
who has spent her full, fragile, throbbing
life with me so please return please
and help me push the cart piled high
with treats for her: my other darling,
my rose-tipped girl, my comfort."

B. A. (Bonnie) St. Andrews, fifty-five, wrote a series of poems called "Your Breast a Unicorn" – from which this section is drawn – in honor of several friends and relatives who have experienced breast cancer.

St. Andrews teaches creative writing and medical humanities at the Center for Bioethics and Humanities in Syracuse, New York. "My students are mainly in nursing and in medicine, and we are affiliated with a teaching hospital and oncology center," she says. "This has allowed me an unparalleled opportunity to witness and salute not only the patients, but also the practitioners. These women and men are truly the human heart of the medical machinery, and they recognize in their patients great dignity, strength, and a nearly miraculous capacity to heal."

St. Andrews also teaches a course in health and gender issues for a consortium of colleges and "has therefore heard moving and eloquent testimony from women of all ages, all backgrounds, and all cultures."

Her poetry has appeared in such publications as Journal of the American Medical Association, Journal of Genetic Counseling, The New Yorker, Journal of General Internal Medicine, *and* The Paris Review.

EMPATHETIC ODE

by Dorothy Stone

This is a poem I never thought I'd writ:
An empathetic ode to a dear friend's tit.

(to be spoken by her)

Oh, little titty,
oh, tickly titty,
I hate to see you go.
I've really grown quite fond of you
you surely ought to know,
as I've watched you change from tiny bud
to gentle mound of snow.
Oh, little titty,
oh, tickly titty,
I hate to see you go.

(to be spoken by me)

I probably should've quit
when I was ahead,
but then I thought of this
last night in bed:
Forgive me this comment
and don't think me flip,
but if God were a woman
you'd have cancer of the hip.

Dorothy Stone thought that Nancy, a good friend and fellow teacher with "a wonderful wit," needed something to lighten her spirits after her breast cancer diagnosis. Stone tucked this poem into Nancy's box at school with a note on the envelope asking her not to open it until she got home. Laughing, Nancy called Stone immediately after reading it to share her positive reaction. Today, Nancy is in remission and doing well.

Recently, Stone reconnected with former student Helen Schary Motro and was thrilled to discover that she, too, would have a poem included in The Cancer Poetry Project. *Motro's poem, "In the Eighties," appears on page 220.*

Stone's poetry has appeared in such publications as Raintown Review, Longfellow Society Journal, ByLine, *and* Poet's Paper.

A retired English teacher, Stone lives with her novelist husband in Concord, Massachusetts. They have a daughter and two granddaughters.

CLAY PIGEONS

by Elizabeth Winthrop

This long slow spring circles round us
like a wary animal. We sniff her,
touch each tulip, drink in each leaf
slipping day by day from red bud
to full summer.

They say the cancer in your brain
looks like a cauliflower upside down
the way it sprouts, shoots out from the central
stem, proliferates, insinuates itself where it doesn't
belong. You have no symptoms yet. You are busy
using your brain as hard as you can
before it turns on you. You are writing wills,
going to the theater, reading great tomes
on weighty subjects, discussing the latest bills
before Congress. You tire friends with your energy
while we hold our breath and cross our fingers
behind our backs.
You speak to me of shark cartilage
and acupuncture and visualization.
You tell me you imagine your brother blasting
away the cauliflower stalks one by one,
the way, with carefully aimed missiles
from his twelve-gauge gun, he knocks clay pigeons
into scattered fragments that rain down on a field
of yellowed corn stubble. Yesterday, you told me
that the gun was growing, had become
a bazooka resting on his hip blowing
things to smithereens. *How does he miss
the brain itself?* I want to ask, but don't.
I want it to work. I want you to be here
when spring comes round next year.
My fingers grow stiff with wishing.

The Cancer Poetry Project

Elizabeth Winthrop, fifty-two, wrote poems during her friend's illness "as a way of trying to comprehend and transmute the experience, perhaps so there would be some of her spirit left after her body had gone, and because I wanted to remember every step of the road that she and I and so many of her friends and family tried to walk with her." Her friend died in October 1995 after a three-year battle with cancer.

Winthrop is a writer of fiction for adults and children. Her latest picture book for children, Promises *(Clarion Books, 2000), tells the story of a little girl who learns to live with her mother's cancer.*

Winthrop, mother of a daughter and son, divides her time between New York City and the Berkshires.

IN THE EIGHTIES

by Helen Schary Motro

You pressed the doctor
for your odds.
"In the 80s," you phone to say.

"He means," I say,
"you'll reach your eighties!"
And I spin for you
a story
how we'll have tea then,
at the Plaza,
and Eloise will come in
with her Social Security check.
And we'll reminisce
how we babysat for
each other's babies
as we choose
undershirts for
our great-grandchildren.
We'll take a cab
to Sheep's Meadow
humming Simon & Garfunkel
and remember taking turns
waiting on a mile-long line
for Shakespeare in the Park.
Under wisteria at the Cloisters
we'll be as old as the displays.

In our eighties, I tell you,
you won't have to rush out anymore
to put quarters in the meter.

But all the while
I am looking at the circles

under your eyes
And thinking of the
unthinkable 20 percent.

"We have been friends since our mid-twenties, when we met through a babysitting co-op," says Helen Schary Motro, fifty-two, of her friend in the poem. "She has opened her heart to me and my family and has stood by me for many years. One way to work through my fears about her cancer, which I could not express to her during her illness, was to explore my feelings through poetry." Motro reports that her friend is still under treatment, but in remission.

Motro's poetry and essays have appeared in such anthologies and journals as Gifts from Our Grandmothers *(Crown Publishing, 2000),* Voices *(Voices Israel, 1999, 2000), and* ZygZag. *She is also an opinion columnist for the* Jerusalem Post, *and her articles have appeared widely in the American press, including* The New York Times, Boston Globe, Baltimore Sun, *and* Christian Science Monitor. *Motro was delighted to reconnect with her former teacher, Dorothy Stone, who contacted her after reading her articles in the* Boston Globe. *Stone's poem, "Empathetic Ode," appears on page 216.*

A lawyer, Motro lives in Israel and New York with her cardiologist husband. They have three daughters. "And yes," she says, "in the poem I refer to Eloise *by Kay Thompson, the fictional little girl who lived in the Plaza Hotel."*

TURBAN

by Suellen Kone Wedmore

After the chemicals
kicked in, she lost her hair –
it came off in her hands like scythed grass,
and even though the doctor said

this would happen – the nausea, the waiting,
the buying of the wig, the watching of faces
on the first bald day – she winced
when friends told her *You look nice this morning.*

Now, when I take her for her treatment
she wears a blue terry cloth turban, cocked slightly
to the right, and she jiggles her earrings – dangling hearts
and pearls – but behind the smile

I see the fear of a diver,
bare toes gauging the spring of a board
high above the pool. In the car
I pick topics carefully: the weather, last night's movie.

What? she asks, distracted, I think, by the taunt
of the unknown. We near the hospital
and she lifts her eyes unhurriedly, tells me
how her son made dean's list in college, how often

her daughter calls . . . and just
when I think she might be bragging, I remember
how I braid my hair,
left strand

over right
over left,
and how when I get to the end

I tie it off with an elastic band.

Suellen Kone Wedmore, fifty-eight, wrote this poem when her friend Casey was undergoing cancer treatment. "I could not believe that her vibrant, generous, fun-loving life might end," Wedmore says. "As I drove Casey to therapy, I could sense fear under her polite conversation. I hurt for her and tried to at least begin to understand that fear."

Poet laureate for the town of Rockport, Massachusetts, Wedmore works as a speech therapist and writer. She is the mother of three grown children, has one granddaughter, and lives with her physician husband in a century-old house a short walk from the sea.

GIFTS

by Patti Marshock

She gives you a present, a little doll, handmade
of empty spools and new buttons, held together with floral wire.
It looks like you: your brown hair, brown eyes,
in a uniform just the color of yours,
wearing a tinsel halo. You look at her fading frame and
wonder why she used her precious time in such a way.

A little narcotic lets her fingers move and work.
Sometimes the sentences don't come out just right,
but they can be repeated later today or
maybe tomorrow. And if she needs it, the dose can
be repeated too, sooner rather than later. She says she
knows because you told her that.

She can make hats, or little model cars, for the child
of her youngest son, due in three months.

She brings these with her in a shopping bag so you can see.
She tells you Ensure milkshakes have a lot of calories, but she
gags on its sweetness. You suggest macaroni and cheese.
She calls you to let you know how good it was and
how much she ate on her anniversary.

She comments on the warm feel of your hands,
as you get ready to puncture her fragile skin,
and how the light shines on your hair as you tuck an
oven-warmed blanket around her feet. She
looks directly into your eyes when you hang
a colorless bag of fluid on the pole beside her.

And you try to tell her how to manage diarrhea, mouth sores,
anorexia, alopecia, fevers, chills, fatigue.
But before all that, she wants to know who you are.

So you give her your credentials: RN, BSN, OCN.
You tell her where you've worked, how much
experience you have, where you went to school.

She wants different details . . . your favorite color,
how long you've been married, where you grew up.
She asks about your kids, how old they are,
whether you'll get a vacation, where you'll go. She wants
to know how much you make for doing this, if you like your job.
Whether it's worth it.

*Patti Marshock, forty-three, has been an oncology nurse for sixteen years.
She currently works in an outpatient chemotherapy unit. "Patients often
give me little presents to show their appreciation for the work I do," she says.
"But their most precious gifts come through their everyday strength and
courage. They show real caring and concern for their families, their friends,
other cancer patients, and yes, even the medical staff. What could be more
beautiful than that?"*

*One day, a friend asked Marshock why she loved her work, and the poem
"Gifts" was born. This is her second published poem. Tad Richards, whose
poem "Elegy" appears on page 92, is her poetry teacher and mentor.*

*A native of Tennessee, Marshock now lives in Phoenix, Arizona, with
her husband of twenty-one years, Tim, and their two teenage daughters,
Laura and Leslie.*

FRIENDS FOR LIFE

by Rochelle Jewel Shapiro

I lie in your bed beside you, run my hand over your scalp.
You look naked without your hair.
You're thirty-four, a year younger than the age your doctor believed
a woman should be tested.
It spread to your lungs.
Your breasts are gone.
You have only a mediport
to pump chemo in.
Every four weeks for the next six months,
you'll be filled like your Land Rover at Amoco.

Listless, cake-lipped, you rest for hours
to have the strength to read
a few pages of Harry Potter to your daughters.
The oldest hears the rasp beneath your soft voice
and pulls herself back as if she happened upon a sorceress.
Her friend's mother died last year even though the "C" word
was never spoken in her house either.

The room is filled with gifts:
self-help tapes, macrobiotic cookbooks,
the names of shamans and Rolfers,
a brochure from a healing spa in Romania,
a certificate entitling you to fax your prayers
to the Wailing Wall, a subscription to *Prevention*.
"It's always the healthy
who are expert at getting well," you say.

 The phone rings. It's your husband.
"He's staying late at the office again," you tell me
as you have each night since you've been home.

What can I do? What can I do?
I get up and make you soup.
I run the water for your children's bath.

"This poem poured out of me as a result of a dear friend's bout with cancer,"
says Rochelle Jewel Shapiro, fifty-three. Shapiro's work has been published in
many literary magazines, including Iowa Review, Negative Capability, *and*
Astarte. *Her essay, "The Medium Has a Message," was published in* The
New York Times. *Her story, "The Wild Russian," appears in* Father:
Famous Writers Celebrate the Bond Between Father and Child *(Pocket*
Books, 2000).

Shapiro makes her living as a psychic with a large private practice and has
been interviewed on many radio shows. She lives in Great Neck, New York.

LINES FOR SPRING

by Rebecca Pierre

Say the word,
and daffodils suddenly uncurl
yellow horns, fighting to be first,
with forsythia a close second. Wisteria
will have its way, as will hyacinth and iris.
All the flowers, in their turns, turn out.
Even indoors, the Easter cactus buds
after ten years of stubbornness.
This, too, is spring.

In this season of greening, your voice
becomes thin as reeds. Reeds promise
cattails. The marsh promises tadpoles,
songs of chorus frogs. Ibis bring
spring to Battery Island in the V
of their flight morning and evening.
I think of deer beside the roadway at night,
eyes shining in headlights. And of the dead one,
body broken in half, head cocked back
as if in agony. Yours will not be agony.
Only each day, less and less of you.
I will bring you daffodils, you will whisper
They are perfect. We will never say goodbye,
we will only say *I love you.*

Rebecca Pierre, fifty-four, met her friend Roberta at a Friends of the Library meeting about three years before Roberta's death at age ninety-one. "I loved her audacity and charm," Pierre says. "We giggled together like girls. It was lovely to tap at her door and know I would be greeted with open arms."

Poems by Pierre have recently appeared in Lullwater Review, Wellspring, ByLine Magazine, Asheville Poetry Review, *and* The Plaza *(Japan). She lives on an island off the coast of North Carolina. Having recently been debilitated by complications from lupus, she is temporarily retired and spends her time writing and making pottery.*

FOR NINA ON HER SIXTEENTH BIRTHDAY

by Donna Pucciani

Nina of the blackberry eyes,
Nina of the voice soft as smoke,
Nina whose small laugh circles
like a wandering star
over doctors' nodding heads,
Nina, tossing cancer over her shoulder
like a feather boa, dancing
on elfin feet into the future –

Nina, who sits in the fourth row, second seat,
the girl with the homerun grades,
Is temporarily sidelined.
Alone in her bedroom,
or perhaps propped on sofa pillows,
she dismisses numb legs, swollen joints,
shakes her aching head, impatient.

Surrounded by her books,
she inks lines on a page,
thin-nibbed, authoritative;
decapitates Macbeth,
tweaks Cyrano's nose,
mourns Holocaust victims
with her survivor's pen.

I bend over her work late at night,
weary, eye-strained, and
draw strength from touching
the paper she writes on.

Donna Pucciani, fifty-two, has written many poems of reflection and mourn-ing for friends and family members who have lost their fight against cancer. But this poem is a favorite, she says, "because it is a poem of hope in honor of one of my high school students who, despite setbacks, is a tremendous inspira-tion to me in her continual fight against cancer."

When Pucciani was unable to attend Nina's sixteenth birthday party, she sent this poem. Today, "Nina is walking unassisted, has her energy back, and is pursuing a full load of classes."

Pucciani's poems have been published in both British and American liter-ary journals, including Karamu, The Cape Rock, *and* Rockford Review. *She currently teaches English at Glenbard North High School and lives with her husband in Wheaton, Illinois.*

THE THIRTEENTH FLOOR

by Davi Walders

Enter the clatter and clutter of the thirteenth
floor. An aquarium bubbles in the chaos of children
under clinical light. This is the land where they
wait, thin as spidery ferns, in wheelchairs hooked

to Critikons feeding nourishment. Vital signs dot
the halls: "Disposal Area," "Phlebotomy Room,"
"I need a hug today." Pandas and Mickey
Mouse sprawl, Clue spews from a broken box. Parents

and grandparents sit among untouched trays, rise
stiffly to coax their tiny wards to examining
rooms. Pagers and phones ring. Loudspeakers call
someone, somewhere. Ask the child why she's crying.

She weeps words of rage at her Snoopy Band-Aid.
Her arm is wet from mourning the all-gone Pocahontases.
She will not speak of her bruises or blond curls
soon to fall, nor of the four years her parents

count by days and hours. You will not see beyond
the hot waiting room, behind swinging doors into
labs that never close, refrigerators filled with
tissue and blood, into computers choked with trials

and databanks, into the work, the work, the work
of piecing fragile bit by bit. Imagine the nausea,
loss of hair, a lung, childhood, a child, the world
of grandparents, foster parents, aunts, uncles,

lovers burying a lost generation and carrying on.
Feel the night sweats, not just from drugs, disease,
but because of earthquakes and shear drops, sudden

plummets in funding, research, hope. This is the country
where a child grieves Pocahontas, the warrior princess,
well-woman flag she wants to raise on her bruised, stuck
arm. Fierce desire fills the room. Look out the window.
This is the height where white geese fly at eye level,

where snow crystals turn to rain, where the sun sometimes
suddenly breaks through. Turn back. This is the land
of doctors, nurses, staff stopping, stooping, scouring
cabinets and pockets, searching for the right Band-Aid.

Desire and determination, passports to the thirteenth
floor, stamped deep and damp, day after day, in a harbor
where a child finally smiles, pointing to Pocahontas
on her raised arm just below a small, sacred fist.

Davi Walders told the Journal of the American Medical Association *(April
17, 1999) that "the right poem at the right moment has a power that can
change one's perspective on life." Walders developed and directs the Vital
Signs Poetry Project at the National Cancer Institute, part of the National
Institutes of Health (NIH) in Bethesda, Maryland. Funded by The Witter
Bynner Foundation for Poetry, the Vital Signs Poetry Project brings poets,
poetry, and writing opportunities to the parents and guardians of children
who are being treated for life-threatening illnesses. "Poetry has enhanced my
insight and attention to detail, it has increased my compassion for the
human condition, and it has given me courage." Walders hopes the Vital
Signs Poetry Project will do the same for its participants. She wrote this
poem about her experience teaching on the thirteenth floor of the NIH clinic.
    Walders lives in Chevy Chase, Maryland, with her husband of thirty-plus
years. They have two grown daughters.*

THE DAUGHTER, THE MOON AND JAMAICA

by Kate Gray

Better me, she said, *than someone else who has
a family.* At twenty-four she does not orbit
anyone, a globe spinning in a pinball of planets.

All she has left of her father is the necklace of beads
he carved for her birth, each a blessing strung
in set order, repeated in whispers like a rosary, hailing
women, hailing grace, a pendant of a banyan tree dangling
in the middle. Bad luck comes when ties break. Four days

before she heard *cancer* and *terminal,* the pendant dropped.
What she really wants is thick hair, black and curly, her blood
link to Jamaica. Now bald and blue-eyed she could be any
Anglo girl, at least one on the fast track through chemo.

Top scientist for NASA, her mother designed rockets
to transport men to the moon, the only night-light guiding
her in Florida. But now the mother lives as far away
as the moon, turned from a daughter shot with light.

Wherever the daughter lives, she keeps water near to see
the moon reflecting, as if the light might be her mother but more
forgiving, a planet on a constant path, not a comet, the white ball
cradled in her palm, more vibrant than bones turned cheese.

If she were a weed, if the weed grew like her cancer, she might
grow everywhere, her seed slipping from creases of clothes worn
by travelers like her parents, dropping onto tarmacks, train
tracks, in gravel along roads leading away from her. Surely
the world would bloom with flowers opening to the moon.

The Cancer Poetry Project

Kate Gray, now forty, attended the Phi Theta Kappa Honors Institute in Washington, D.C., as a seminar leader in June 1999. "In the midst of five hundred students from community colleges around the nation, one woman stood out," Gray says. "She was bald. Other students flocked to her. I knew immediately that she was a chemo kid, and I gravitated toward her just to check if she needed anything. Her humor, her caring, her perceptiveness, and her incredibly sharp intellect compelled me to gather her story. At the age of twenty-four, this professional triathlete had awakened one day with a blue foot — which eventually led to the diagnosis of a rare bone cancer. She was given three months to live, and I am glad to say that she is still alive, having graduated from her community college. She is now teaching physical education in an elementary school and is feeling well. We still talk once a week."

An English instructor at a community college in Portland, Oregon, Gray won a chapbook contest last year and published her first collection of poems, Where She Goes *(Blue Light Press, 2000). Every day she gets up at dawn to write and walk along the Columbia River with her two golden retrievers.*

HIKING IN THE ANZA-BORREGO DESERT AFTER SURGERY
For Liz

by Francine Sterle

So much died here last year
but last month rain forced
peach-red mouths out of balding sand,
and within weeks sun coaxed
tiny constellations of yellow,
purple, and white into sandy flats,
along rocky dirt roads,
deep into Blair Valley, up through
Yaqui Pass, and what was once
simple misery shifted
beneath a thick cover of flowering
fiddlenecks and brittlebush,
chuparosa, ocotillo, desert tobacco.
What a place to find myself
after the doctor's diagnosis
left its scar as if a cactus spine
had been dragged across my chest.
I will never be the same
knowing how effortlessly death
rests in the cells of my body,
yet with each step I am willing
to say yes to the chances I take,
to the hope no one can take from me
here in the midst of my recovery
now that I've seen what can thrive
in the bankrupt landscape of the heart.

Francine Sterle, forty-eight, wrote this poem in the voice of a dear friend who had been treated for breast cancer in her late thirties. "I was trying to come to terms with her experience," Sterle explains. After a seven-year remission, her friend was diagnosed with and treated for lung cancer, then, in 2000, she was diagnosed with liver, bone, and brain cancer. Her prognosis is not hopeful. "It seems hideously unfair. I am heartbroken and filled with a deep, deep grief."

Sterle's poetry has been published in such literary journals as Nimrod, North American Review, The Beloit Poetry Journal, *and* Atlanta Review. *Her books include* The White Bridge *(Poetry Harbor, 1999) and* Every Bird Is One Bird *(Tupelo Press, 2001).*

Sterle lives in northern Minnesota with psychologist husband Jonathan Speare, three geriatric cats, and a two-year-old Rhodesian ridgeback hound.

SNATCHING

by Christopher Gutkind

snatches of speech one flight up   the old
are playing with gadgets   cancer toys
with pumps and buttons   insertions instructions
that the young devised

it's all so serious now   it's all to the end
to the prize   life   detaching without any time for us
looking back   in surprise at our surprise

how could it be over how could it be   the
final over   nothing left but leftovers
people places things   playthings we took   up
still talking   gossiping good

For four years Christopher Gutkind, now thirty-eight, lived in a London flat under his landlady, an old family friend named Christian Ness. "She was among the first women to graduate from the Architectural Association, and she was always searching and learning, thinking about the world. In the short time that I knew her, she took up sculpture. I used to see her puttering about the garden, working on one of her creations one moment and gardening the next. Her life and her spirit moved me even then. They moved me to write this poem." Ness died of liver cancer in 1993 at age seventy-seven, after fighting the illness for a year and a half.

Gutkind was born in The Hague, grew up in Montreal, lived in London for many years, and now lives in Berkeley, California, where he works as a librarian.

APARTMENT ON THIRD AND BROOKS
Hillcrest, California
Sunday, May 20, 1996

by Kjersti Reed

I hear Glenn below my open
window, talking to Marty and Lora –
he says he had a stone dragon
stolen from his porch last September
but he epoxied this one down
"so it'll be here after I'm gone,"
his deep slow laugh tumbling.
Then I hear Miranda ask him
in her scratchy three-year-old
voice: "Why is that purple stuff
on your legs?" I mumble
Don't answer in my head,
imagine her parents' young
faces, a ruby chagrin
tattooing their cheeks.
Glenn says, "Because I have
cancer, that's why."
Silence climbs thorny bougainvillaea
arching papery magenta bracts
over the walkway. Then goodbyes.
Glenn tells them have a nice day.
He's out there drilling, attaching
everything to the wrought-iron fence
of his porch with cable so it will
stay put; even his new patio table
pressed up against brown blotchy
stucco gets tethered, chairs pushed in.
I hear him drilling now again – when
I leave today I'll see what he's securing
for the future.

GLENN'S LAUGH
Sunday, July 28, 1996

by Kjersti Reed

Glenn's whitecaps of bombastic
laughter roll on and on from
his flat, not like I thought
one with Kaposi's might laugh,
a belly-rocking rapture from a man
who knows the moment he lives in,
reeling as he is from a long winter
of coughing, then blinking
into a spring he didn't expect.
I watch his bleach-
blonde hair shine to white gold
as he rolls out a chipped blue
ten-speed from the doorless shed, pedals
down our steep hill to his doctor's.
Today, I wonder does he also laugh
like that because he knows
its power, hilarity's footfall
more sprightly than death's.
Glen is no dummy,
he shares with Norman Cousins
the empirical study of the dance
of mind with body. So maybe his chortling
is not just for joy or fear
but an elixir for health, that crown
we don't know sits on our head
until it's wobbly.

"I'm inspired to write about people who move me, who embrace life through so many difficulties," says Kjersti Reed, *fifty-eight, who has written quite a few poems about her friend and neighbor, Glenn. "He rides a motorcycle, he's full of life – he's no quitter, this guy."*

An award-winning poet whose work has been published in such journals as Kalliope, Pearl, *and* Press, *Reed has a new chapbook,* Notes on a Broken Chandelier *(March Street Press, 2000).*

Reed lives with partner Robb in San Diego, where she teaches writing at the University of San Diego and at Southwestern College. She has three children: Ben, Doug, and Jill.

GOOD NIGHT

by Jo Nelson

All week she was at the dying.
Slow, laborious, her breath caught
rose and caught.
"Ride the wind," I sang to her
but my touch did not help her pass.
I opened the windows to rain song,
let the breeze tease her ribs,
scrambled her eggs and lamb rice.
Last night she did not eat.

Month by month she shut down –
eyes, ears, nose –
the last month, she hardly heard my footsteps
on wooden stairs
but she followed the scent of her food
or my voice as I called her to it.
Two years I stayed by her
after cancer tunneled her down to one room.
"Let go, Sasha," I chanted
but long as she heard me, she fought.

It was a good night for dying.
The moon was full enough
to cast shadows on the floor.
A comet trailed the dog star.
Outside, toms serenaded.
On the radio, Monk.

Jo Nelson, fifty-five, joined a few friends in caring for an elderly friend who was slowly dying of pancreatic cancer, which went untreated for too long. "She had no family left and wanted to die at home," Nelson says. "Though she didn't want us to prolong her life, she wasn't quite ready to give up, and it took a long time."

Over the last ten years, many of Nelson's friends have either died from or successfully fought cancer. "Writing is how I grieve for them or celebrate their renewed health," she says.

Nelson's poetry and prose have been widely published in national magazines and anthologies. Her chapbook, A Taste of Light *(Ye Olde Font Shoppe), was released in 2000, and another is forthcoming from Pudding House Press.*

Nelson currently writes, teaches creative writing classes, and cares for a host of critters on her small farm in Gig Harbor, Washington.

WALK ME INTO THE MORNING

by Beth Shorr Jaffe

Just rest, she whispers
serving me tea in bed
Just   Rest
The words melt above me
Her face staring at my eyes
that now can speak
with a blink
  So close, I smell her resolve
to hold onto daylight
Today she came to me
wanting me to play
  Can we ring around the rosy?
I am her mother
I breathe
so her prayer will be granted
I blink dry eyes
She reads them:
  Come hold my hand
I feel her
fingers young and smooth
wanting us as we were
  Please spin and dance with me?

Tomorrow, the answer
that comes from outside,
from a place I cannot name,
will bring us peace
  Watching each other
we will nod   Let go
One Two
Buckle my shoe
Holding her breath
Up and up I'll float,

catching stars
to sprinkle in her heart
Catching light
to shine on her loveliness

Release your salty sting
and sweetness of tears
Smile for me your heavenly smile
Let go
I promise I will hold you in me
I promise I will be your mother
Always,

Now promise
to walk me into the morning

Beth Shorr Jaffe, forty-eight, works as a full-time writer, except on Thursdays. Every Thursday for the past six years, she has volunteered at a community cancer center. Jaffe wrote this poem in the voice of a mother with lung cancer saying goodbye to her daughter. "I watched these two women love each other through a two-year ordeal until their farewell," says Jaffe. "As I offered small comforts, they reached right back out to offer tenderness and comfort in return. They brought me great sadness and tremendous, everlasting joy." This is her first published poem.

Jaffe has two essays in the Simon and Schuster Chocolate for the Soul *series, a short fiction piece forthcoming in* Kalliope, *and two novels currently represented by Sterling Lord Literistic. She lives in Short Hills, New Jersey, with her husband and two sons.*

AN ONCOLOGY NURSE'S TRIBUTE

by Barbara Hunt, RN, BSN

In your struggle to fight cancer
You have let me come alongside
To hear your hurts
To answer your questions
To hold your hand
To cry and laugh with you

My life is richer
My love for life is stronger
My reason for living is clearer
Because of you.

Barbara Hunt, forty-four, has worked as an oncology nurse for eighteen years. She is currently employed at Midwestern Regional Medical Center in Zion, Illinois. "Much of what my patients are dealing with is difficult to talk about," Hunt says. "When I share my poetry with them, it opens doors and allows me to give emotional and spiritual support in ways that would not normally be available to me. I wrote this poem to acknowledge the positive impact my patients have had on my life, and to thank them." This is her first published poem.

Hunt is married, has three children, and is currently pursuing a master's degree in nursing with an emphasis on education.

FOR A FRIEND LYING IN INTENSIVE CARE WAITING FOR HER WHITE BLOOD CELLS TO REJUVENATE AFTER A BONE MARROW TRANSPLANT

For Judy

by Barbara Crooker

The jonquils. They come back. They split the earth with
      their green swords, bearing cups of light.
The forsythia comes back, spraying its thin whips with
      blossom, one loud yellow shout.
The robins. They come back. They pull the sun on the
      silver thread of their song.
The iris come back. They dance in the soft air in silken
      gowns of midnight blue.
The lilacs come back. They trail their perfume like a scarf
      of violet chiffon.
And the leaves come back, on every tree and bush, millions
      and millions of small green hands applauding your return.

---

*Barbara Crooker, fifty-five, wrote this poem for a former neighbor and
close friend, whose friendship continued even after she moved halfway
across the country to Wisconsin. Her friend died at age forty-four after a
three-year fight with cancer.*

    *"She had this poem pasted up by her bed in the isolation room after her
bone marrow transplant," Crooker says. "I ended up writing a twenty-one-
poem cycle about her struggle. She taught me a great deal about living in the
present and living life to its fullest, even while she was dying." Crooker's
poems will soon be published as a chapbook called* The White Poems
(Barnwood Press, 2001).

    *Crooker won the New Millennium Writing's Y2K Award and the
Dancing Poetry Competition, both in 2000. She lives in rural northeastern
Pennsylvania with her husband and son, and has two grown daughters.*

Acknowledgment for Previously Published Work:

"Double Mastectomy" by Ann Campanella, first published in *Award Winning Poems,* North Carolina Poetry Society. "Self-Examination" by Clinton B. Campbell, first published in *Exit 13*. "For a Friend Lying in the Intensive Care Waiting for Her White Blood Cells to Rejuvenate" by Barbara Crooker, first published in *Poets On.* "The cancerous cell" by James Doyle, first published in *The Ohio Review.* "March 29, 1985" and "The Seven Sorrows" by Nancy Madison Fitzgerald, first published in *A Creature Who Belongs* (Poetry Harbor, 1998), used with permission. "Cigarettes" by Suzanne Frischkorn, first published in *JAMA.* "Lucky" by Tony Gloeggler, first published in *The Ledge*. "Survival Diptych" by David Graham, first published in David Graham's chapbook, *Stutter Monk* (Flume Press, Forest Ranch, California), in 2000, used with permission. "Odds" by Jane Eaton Hamilton, first published in *Body Rain* (Brick Books, 1991), used with permission. "Reconstruction" by Lisa Katz, first published in *Nimrod.* "Midnight in the Pretty Little House" by Greg Keith, first published in *Life Near 310 Kelvin* (SLG Books, 1998), used with permission. "The Answer" by Bonnie Maurer, first published in *Nimrod.* "Let Us Now Praise" by Judith McComb, first published in *Bridge.* "The Diagnosis" by Majid Mohiuddin, first published in *JGIM.* "One Hundred and Ten Days" and "Variations on My Room in the Bone Marrow Unit: In the Room of Cows" by Julie Moulds, first published in *The Woman with a Cubed Head* (New Issues Poetry Press, 1998), reprinted with permission. "Impotence" by Harvey Overton, first published in *How We Measure Fourteen and Other Poems* (Hidkey Press, 1998), used with permission. "Apartment on Third and Brooks" by Kjersti Reed, first published in *Pearl*. "Elegy" by Tad Richards, first published in *My Night with the Language Thieves* (Victoria, 2001), used with permission. "She Asked for a Joke or Poem" by Charles Rossiter, first published in *Journal of Poetry Therapy.* "Mother Eulogy" by Shannon Sexton, first published in *Inside Grief* (Wise Press, 2001), used with permission. "In Remission" by Floyd Skloot, first published in *The Sewanee Review.* "Seed" by Floyd Skloot, first published in *The Hudson Review.* "How to Stay Alive" by Judith Strasser, first published in *Prairie Schooner.* "Say Yes" by Marc J. Straus, first published in *Symmetry* (Copyright © 2000 by Marc J. Straus. Published 2000. All rights reserved.), used with permission from the publisher, Northwestern University Press. "Garden Variety" by Colette Giles Tennant, first published in *The Anthology of New England Writers.* "Slow Dancing at the Med-Inn" by F. Richard Thomas, reprinted with permission from *Death at Camp Pahoka* (Michigan State University Press, East Lansing, Michigan, 2000). "The Thirteenth Floor" by Davi Walders, first published in *JAMA.* "Turban" by Suellen Kone Wedmore, first published in *Byline.* "The Wrong Month" by Anthony Russell White, first published in *How I Learned about Baseball* (Talent House Press, 2000), used with permission. "Shape Shifter" by Scott Wiggerman, first published in *Vegetables and Other Relationships* (Plain View Press, 2000), used with permission. "Because a world may be called into being" by Gary Young, first published in *Braver Deeds* (Gibbs Smith, 1999), used with permission. "A Man Learning Women" by David Zeiger, first published in *Life on My Breath* (David Zeiger, 1995).